Glamify Your Goal

Challenge Yourself to Achieve One Epic Goal in Just Ninety Days

(Workbook and Planner Inside)

ROSEANNE BAKER

GLAMIFY YOUR GOAL

Challenge Yourself to Achieve One Epic Goal in Just Ninety Days

(*Workbook and Planner Inside*)

---By---
ROSEANNE BAKER
Founder *of Breakthrough Empire*™

Copyright © 2017 by ROSEANNE BAKER. All Rights Reserved

Licensing Notes

All rights reserved under U.S. and International copyright law. This book may not be copied, scanned, digitally reproduced, or printed for resale, may not be uploaded on shareware or free sites, or used in manner except quoting of brief excerpt for the purpose of promotion or articles without the express permission of the author. Although every precaution has been taken in preparation of this book, the distributor and author assume no responsibility for omissions, inaccuracy, or errors. Neither is any liability assumed for damages resulting from the information contained in this book.

For permissions requests, write to author at: hi@roseannebaker.com or visit: http://www.roseannebaker.com

Disclaimer

The examples, strategies, and advice contained in this book may not be suitable for every person or situation. The materials contained in this book are not intended to guarantee or represent you will achieve your desired results, and the author and distributor make no such guarantee. Success is determined by many factors beyond the control of the author and the distributor including, but not limited to effort levels and time. You understand that business ideas and others carry an inherent risk of loss of capital or failure. Neither the distributor or the author shall be liable for damages arising therefrom. This book is not intended to provide any legal or financial advice. You should utilize competent personnel for financial and legal guidance to evaluate any business or other specific idea.

The author and the distributor assume no responsibility for your actions. The author of this book does not provide medical advice or prescribe the use of any technique as a form of treatment for emotional, physical, or medical problems without the advice of a physician. The author's intent is only to offer information of a general nature.

Cover Design: Maria Carmen Soy

Edited By: Robin J. Samuels

ISBN: 978-0-692-91554-7

Glamify Your Goal

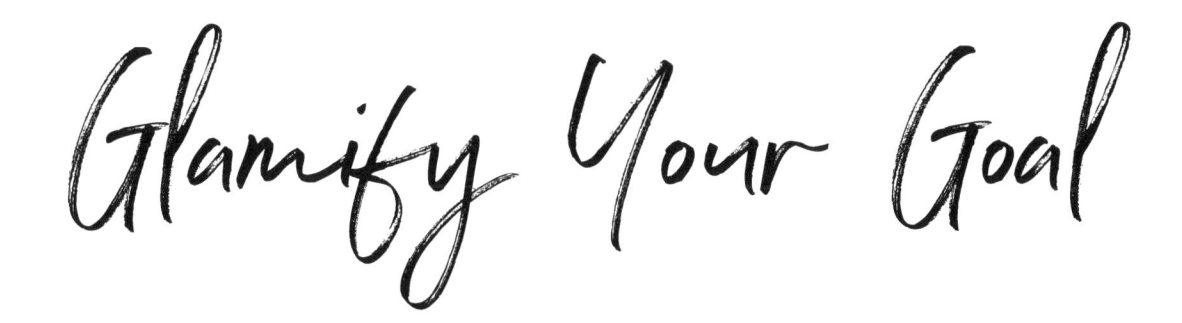

THIS BOOK

BELONGS TO THE FABULOUS

_____

If found, please call: _____

DEDICATION

This book is dedicated to *you*.

The opportunity to consciously design your life is always glittering before you and it's up to you to do something about it. So, open up your eyes to the wildly beautiful possibilities, always believe in your magnificent self, and take hold of the reins of your life so you can guide your destiny in a direction you desire. May this book inspire and motivate you to take massive action so that you will see your dream or goal come to light and ultimately create a life that truly sparkles. ♥

CONTENTS

She Designs Her Life	xiii
Introduction	xvii

◆◆◆◆◆◆◆◆◆◆◆◆ SECTION 1 ◆◆◆◆◆◆◆◆◆◆◆◆

AUTHENTICALLY YOU

Crystal Vision	3
Uncovering Core Values	5
Explore Your Passions	7
Crafting Your Mission	9
Goal Collection	10

◆◆◆◆◆◆◆◆◆◆◆◆ SECTION 2 ◆◆◆◆◆◆◆◆◆◆◆◆

DESIGN YOUR GLAMOROUS GOAL

What's Your Goal?	15
Get Specific	15
Goal Work Time	16
Measure it, Gorgeous	17
Glam it Up	18

♦♦♦♦♦♦♦♦♦♦ SECTION 3 ♦♦♦♦♦♦♦♦♦♦

SLAYING OBSTACLES

Use the Past to Your Advantage	25
Discover Internal Blocks	26
Uncover External Obstacles	30
Your Dazzling Resources	32

♦♦♦♦♦♦♦♦♦♦ SECTION 4 ♦♦♦♦♦♦♦♦♦♦

GET A FABULOUS MINDSET

Change Your Thinking, Change Your Life	37
The Magic of Complete Responsibility	39
N.O. Means Next Opportunity	41
Mini Vision Board	42
Affirmations for Success	44

♦♦♦♦♦♦♦♦♦♦ SECTION 5 ♦♦♦♦♦♦♦♦♦♦

QUITTING IS NOT AN OPTION

Emergency Action Plan	47
The Power of Joy	48

♦♦♦♦♦♦♦♦♦♦ SECTION 6 ♦♦♦♦♦♦♦♦♦♦

THE GOAL-GETTER PLAN

Goal Mind Map	51
The Success Blueprint	53
Tips for Productivity, Planning, & Success	56

◆◆◆◆◆◆◆◆◆◆◆ SECTION 7 ◆◆◆◆◆◆◆◆◆◆◆

THE GOAL PLANNER

How to Use the Planner	61
Declare Your Goal	63
Set Your Mini Goals	65

ROUND ONE: DAYS 1–10

Mini Goal Planner	66
Daily Action Plan	67
Reflection	77

ROUND TWO: DAYS 11–20

Mini Goal Planner	79
Daily Action Plan	80
Reflection	90

ROUND THREE: DAYS 21–30

Mini Goal Planner	92
Daily Action Plan	93
Reflection	103

ROUND FOUR: DAYS 31–40

Mini Goal Planner	105
Daily Action Plan	106
Reflection	116

ROUND FIVE: DAYS 41–50

Mini Goal Planner	118
Daily Action Plan	119
Reflection	129

ROUND SIX: DAYS 51–60

Mini Goal Planner	131
Daily Action Plan	132
Reflection	142

ROUND SEVEN: DAYS 61–70

Mini Goal Planner	144
Daily Action Plan	145
Reflection	155

ROUND EIGHT: DAYS 71–80

Mini Goal Planner	157
Daily Action Plan	158
Reflection	168

ROUND NINE: DAYS 81–90

Mini Goal Planner	170
Daily Action Plan	171

◆◆◆◆◆◆◆◆◆◆◆◆ SECTION 8 ◆◆◆◆◆◆◆◆◆◆◆◆

CELEBRATE YOU

Celebrating Your Journey	183
What Happens Now?	186

MY GIFT TO YOU

Want a wall planner to dazzle up your goal setting all year long?
Get my FREE wall planner template.

DOWNLOAD HERE:

http://www.breakthroughempire.com/glamifygift

She Designs Her Life

She owns her dreams and is never afraid to dream big.
She knows what she wants and why she wants it.
She knows the direction she's heading.

To her, "failure" is not the end but a new beginning,
a sign that she needs to re-design her plan.

She doesn't let fear stop her, and instead faces it with grace,
because she knows her dreams are on the other side of her fear.

She sees obstacles as an opportunity to grow.

She deserves greatness and has the confidence to go for what she wants.
She knows she's the only one responsible for showing up for her goals,
and for making them a reality.

So, she does...

She has a big vision. A goal. A written plan.
She takes action. Stays consistent.
Most importantly, she never gives up.

She designs her life.
She's unstoppable.

-ROSEANNE BAKER

INTRODUCTION

"Be the author of your life so you can write your own fairy tale."

–ROSEANNE BAKER

#GlamifyYourGoal

INTRODUCTION

"There is an abundance of opportunity glittering all around you."

As you opened this book just now you unearthed a secret passage to the path of infinite possibilities. I am glowing with excitement as I write this because I know that you are about to accomplish something wonderful!

In the next ninety days, I want you to challenge yourself to achieve something *epic*—something huge that will WOW you! You might know exactly what your goal is, or have lots of dreams or goals in mind to choose from, or maybe you don't know yet what you want to achieve. Either way, this workbook is for you. As you complete the exercises in this book, you'll determine one goal to accomplish and style it so that it's glamorous to *you*. Then create a plan that will enable you to take massive action toward accomplishing it.

I believe you discovered this book because you are ready to accomplish something *amazing*! It takes *tons* of courage to step outside your comfort zone to make things happen, and you are making a conscious decision to do that. Not everyone is willing do the hard work that it takes to get what they want, and the fact that you chose this book makes you special, girl! There is an abundance of opportunity glittering all around you. Can you feel it, gorgeous?

GET READY TO GLAM IT UP, GIRL!

This book is so much more than *just* a workbook and planner to achieve a goal. Some other benefits you can expect from this book are that you will:

- Gain undeniable clarity about what you *really* want in life
- Discover your life's purpose
- Identify the obstacles that have been holding you back (and learn how to slay them)
- Experience greater levels of energy, joy, and motivation
- Develop a mindset for future success…and more

A BIT ABOUT GOAL SETTING

Before you dive in to the workbook, I want to talk just a bit about goal setting and why I chose a ninety-day time crunch.

A goal without a written plan is only a wish. When you literally write your goal down on paper, it will feel more real and attainable. That's where this book comes in. When you have a written plan, you'll develop a laser focus because you know exactly what you want, when you want to achieve it by, and have a concrete plan of action for how you are going to achieve it. You'll have a roadmap that leads to your destination.

I chose ninety days because it is enough time to accomplish a massive goal without losing momentum. Have you ever told yourself you would start working on a goal, "next month," or "this year," or "someday," but you *never* got around to it? We all have done this. But here's the kicker: if you don't give yourself a deadline to accomplish your goal, then the time can expand for as long as you give yourself to complete it.

The type of goal that you set is *so* important. Sometimes we set goals that don't serve us because they:

- Don't align with who we are and may lead us in a direction that we don't want to go
- Are not something we really want, but what others want for us
- Aren't where our passions truly lie
- Don't motivate or electrify us

None of these things will happen with this book. Nope! We'll *glamify*—or "glam up"— your goal, meaning that it will align with your passions, your visions, with who you really are, and will ultimately lead you in the direction you want your life to go. Glamming up your goal will rev you up because you'll have an undeniable reason *why* you want to achieve it. *Annnnd* when you achieve a glamorous goal, you'll add a spark of fabulousness to your life too! So, challenge yourself and you'll make amazing things happen, girl!

HOW THIS BOOK IS DESIGNED

SECTION ONE – AUTHENTICALLY YOU
You'll gain clarity on your:
- ideal future
- core values
- passions
- mission
- dreams and goals that you desire

SECTION TWO – DESIGN YOUR GLAMOROUS GOAL

- You'll choose one large goal to smash with the workbook
- Style your goal so it's meaningful to *you* and will skyrocket your motivation

SECTION THREE – SLAYING OBSTACLES

- Discover past, present, and possible future obstacles that might keep you from achieving your goal
- You'll get unstuck before you start your journey by determining where your current mindset is and conquer fears and obstacles
- Explore resources that can help you along the way

SECTION FOUR – GET A FABULOUS MINDSET

- Discover the beliefs you have about yourself and why taking responsibility matters
- Create uplifting affirmations and a vison board

SECTION FIVE – QUITTING IS NOT AN OPTION

A handy resource if times get tough. This section will help you:

- find a solution to a problem
- uplift your mood if you are having a bad day

SECTION SIX – THE GOAL-GETTER PLAN

- Clarify and map out the steps required to achieve your goal using the *Goal Mind Map* and *The Success Blueprint*

SECTION SEVEN – THE GOAL PLANNER

This is the planner section where you'll create your action plan for the next ninety days.

The planner includes:

- Nine 10-Day Rounds. Break down your large goal into small bite-sized goals so you'll gain more clarity, momentum, and earn small wins along the way
- Daily Action Planner for each of the ninety days
- Reflection questions at the end of each round

There are powerful questions throughout the planner pages that'll help you stay unstuck, keep you revved up, and on track to crush your goal.

SECTION EIGHT – CELEBRATE YOU
- Celebrate and reflect on all of your wonderful accomplishments

IMPORTANT

I'm sure you are excited to start working on your goal, and may be tempted to skip some sections in the workbook, but please don't girlfriend! All the exercises in this workbook build upon each other. It is organized to help you design your goal in the best possible way. Allow yourself sufficient time to complete the exercises, ok? You deserve it!

MAKE IT HAPPEN!

You possess the power to have, be, and do anything that your heart truly desires. You just have to want it badly enough, believe that it's possible for you, get a written plan in place, work hard for it, and BAM! Anything you desire can be *all* yours.

To your success,

xx Roseanne

P.S. Visit http://www.breakthroughempire.com to share your glamorous goal and your experience throughout this exciting journey.

P.P.S. Wherever you see this mini diamond image, ♦ you'll get tips or free bonuses that go along with this workbook. Before you start, you can access your bonuses here: http://www.breakthroughempire.com/glamifybonuses

Ready to Achieve Awesomeness?!

Let's go girl...

SECTION 1

Authentically You

> "Decide what you really want, then align your goals to mirror it."

—ROSEANNE BAKER

#GlamifyYourGoal

CRYSTAL VISION

Do you believe that your life happens *to* you, or that you have a part in designing your reality? One thing I hope you come to realize while using this workbook is that you *can* deliberately style your life. Setting and achieving *glamorous* goals that align with where you want your life to go will ultimately move you toward your ideal future.

In order to get what you desire and to live a life that fully sparkles, you need to know what you want. I like to think about this in terms of five years because it is not too far away, but not too close either.

Find a quiet space where you won't be disturbed. Make yourself a cup of matcha tea (or a drink that you love), put on relaxing music, light a candle, or whatever gets you into the "deep thinking zone." Do this now, I'll wait. ☺

So, what do you *really* want in your life? For this exercise, I want you to write what your ideal life would be like five years from now in the eight categories on the next page. Write in the present tense, like it's happening now (ex: "I'm now earning $10,000 per month," or, "I'm walking up the stairs to my beach house and I can smell the salt in the ocean air..."). Close your eyes and vividly imagine... Take time with this. What does your life look like? The scents? How do you feel? Who are you with? Where are you?

Write as if there are no limits to what's possible. Oh, and to be clear, this is what *you* want and not someone else's dreams that you absorbed. Keep in mind that this is not set in stone and your ideal future could change from year to year. Right now, it is important to know what you are working toward so that you can end up where you ultimately want to be. On your mark...get set...go...

GLAMIFY YOUR GOAL

RELATIONSHIPS/ROMANCE/FAMILY	HEALTH

FINANCES	SPIRITUAL

CAREER/SUCCESSES/EDUCATION	LIFESTYLE/RECREATIONAL/TRAVEL/ADVENTURE

CONTRIBUTIONS/CHARITY	MATERIAL ITEMS

Guess what? You've just discovered what your ideal life looks like, which should be the foundation for your goal setting. When you live a life that aligns with your authentic self, your life will illuminate with happiness and meaning.

WHAT NEEDS TO HAPPEN FROM THIS MOMENT ON FOR YOU TO LIVE YOUR IDEAL LIFE?

___

___

___

___

___

___

___

___

___

UNCOVERING CORE VALUES

A value is a personal choice you make on what is important to you and how you ultimately live your life. It is literally the foundation that supports what you do and don't do. If you don't live according to your core values, you will feel unhappy and unfulfilled.

Knowing your core values is like having a guide or a compass to help lead the way. Things you might value are: health, family, friends, career, wealth, community, creativity, or free time. When you discover what your core values are, this will help you realize what your top goals in life should be and keep you on track for living your best life.

WHAT DO YOU STAND FOR?

_____
_____
_____
_____
_____
_____
_____

WHAT WON'T YOU TOLERATE OR WHAT UPSETS YOU?

_____
_____
_____
_____
_____
_____
_____

WHO OR WHAT DO YOU HOLD CLOSE TO YOUR HEART AND WHY?

_____
_____
_____
_____
_____
_____
_____

EXPLORE YOUR PASSIONS

We're the most joyous and fulfilled when we do what we love. What are you passionate about? It could be one thing or you could be multi-passionate. Passions could include hobbies, a particular career, or working for a cause you believe in.

WHAT SPECIAL GIFTS OR TALENTS DO OTHERS SAY YOU HAVE?

_____
_____
_____
_____
_____
_____
_____
_____

WHAT GIVES YOU THE MOST JOY?

_____
_____
_____
_____
_____
_____
_____
_____

WHAT WOULD YOU DO ALL DAY EVERY DAY IF YOU COULD?

_____
_____
_____
_____
_____
_____
_____
_____
_____

WHAT DO YOU WANT YOUR LEGACY TO BE?

_____
_____
_____
_____
_____
_____
_____
_____

HOW DO YOU WANT TO MAKE OTHERS FEEL?

_____
_____
_____

CRAFTING YOUR MISSION

Now that you know what you value and what your passions are, let's create your mission statement. This will help capture the essence of a life you truly desire for yourself, what you want to achieve, and what you believe in. This statement will best describe your life's purpose. There is no right or wrong way to do this.

Considering your answers in the previous sections, how would you best sum up your calling? Write it below.

WHAT'S YOUR MISSION?

My mission in life is to inspire women to live fabulous lives.

My life's calling is to protect and rescue animals.

_____

_____

WHAT SERVICE OR ACTIVITY IS YOUR MISSION URGING YOU TO PURSUE?

_____

_____

_____

_____

_____

_____

_____

GOAL COLLECTION

Write down big dreams or goals you want to accomplish in the next one to five years in each of the eight categories. Write these desires in the present tense as if they are true now. Imagine your dreams and goals as if you are watching them unfold in front of you.

This exercise has a few rules:

- This is all about *you,* girlfriend.

- It's not about what others want for you or expect from you. These are things that *you* want. I want you to write things that illuminate *your* heart.

- These goals do not have to make sense to anyone else, just to you. Even if these are goals that others may not approve of or may think are unrealistic.

- Don't be afraid to dream BIG with no limits. You are reaching beyond the stars here.

Be mindful of bursts of joy or excitement you feel about particular goals because these are speaking the most strongly to your heart. Any time you think of a big dream or goal you can write it here; this way you always have all of your desires in one place. Take it away, lovely…

ROSEANNE BAKER

RELATIONSHIPS/ROMANCE/FAMILY	HEALTH

FINANCES	SPIRITUAL

CAREER/SUCCESSES/EDUCATION	LIFESTYLE/RECREATIONAL/TRAVEL/ADVENTURE

CONTRIBUTIONS/CHARITY	MATERIAL ITEMS

SECTION 2

Design Your Glamorous Goal

"The more you glam up your goal, the more motivated you'll be to accomplish it."

-ROSEANNE BAKER

#GlamifyYourGoal

WHAT'S YOUR GOAL?

Go back and review the values, passions, mission statement, and goals you wrote on the last few pages. You now have a clear vision of which goals align with your ideal life. Now circle all the goals you'd like to have accomplished one year from now. Pick one of these goals that you would like to achieve or work toward achieving in the next ninety days. This goal should get you excited, be outside your comfort zone, and be something that you truly want to accomplish. This is NOT a goal you're trying to accomplish to please someone else.

WHAT'S YOUR AMAZING GOAL?

What excites you and makes you feel pumped up just thinking about accomplishing it?
Think about which goal might have the greatest positive impact on your life.
Which would be the most realistic to pursue at this time?

GET SPECIFIC

Woohoo, you've decided on a goal! Now, let's make that goal *really* specific. A specific goal will state the exact target result so you know when you achieved it. A non-specific goal would be, "I'll write a book." An example of a specific goal is, "I'll write a goal-setting workbook."

WHAT SPECIFIC GOAL WILL YOU ACHIEVE IN NINETY DAYS?

Rewrite your goal and be as specific as possible. This will help provide clarity on what you are trying to achieve.

I will...

_____

_____

GOAL WORK TIME

I want you to achieve something epic, but some goals can't be realistically accomplished in ninety days even with consistent, hard work. You should push yourself *just* a bit, but not so much that you will have an unrealistic goal.

If it will take longer than ninety days, you can break up your big goal into a smaller, more doable goal. This way when the deadline arrives, you'll be closer to achieving the larger goal.

Let's say you plan to publish a 100-page self-help workbook. You may realistically be able to write a first draft of the book in ninety days, but not necessarily be able to write the book from scratch *and* publish it in that time frame. So, you could scale this goal down to a smaller goal that you'll write 100 first-draft pages of your workbook in ninety days.

Let's get a rough idea how much time you have available to work toward your goal in the next ninety days. Keep in mind any prior engagements you may have committed to and days you work your 9-5 job, etc. Don't forget to set aside time with family, friends, and for relaxation so you don't get burned out! Be realistic with yourself.

HOW MANY DAYS PER WEEK CAN YOU WORK ON YOUR GOAL?

Ninety days is almost thirteen weeks.

_____ Days

HOW MANY HOURS EACH WEEK CAN YOU DEVOTE TO WORKING ON YOUR GOAL?

_____ Hours

Will this be enough time to achieve your goal? If not, chunk your big goal down to a smaller goal. Keep in mind that you might be able to free up time to work toward your goal for the challenge period. For example, if you are attending a weekly art class, maybe you can miss a few here and there. If you have cleaning or errands to do, hire someone to help you. You can delegate tasks that *you* don't necessarily need to do to free up more time for your goal work. If you need to adjust your goal at this time, go back and do that now.

MEASURE IT, GORGEOUS

Now you've gotta make it measurable, girly. How would someone else know that you smashed your goal? To do this, I want you to make your goal more detailed. Think in terms of numbers, dates, time, etc. How much and by when? For the deadline date, determine when you will start the ninety-day challenge and count up from the start date.

"I will write 100 pages of the first draft of my goal-setting workbook by December 31, 2017."

NOW REWRITE YOUR GOAL AGAIN TO BE AS SPECIFIC AND MEASURABLE AS POSSIBLE.

I will...

_____

_____

GLAM IT UP

Alrighty, gorgeous, now you are going to take your fabulous goal you just set and glitter it with some *serious* glamification. Ready? Let's glamify...

HOW DOES THIS GOAL ALIGN WITH YOU?

Your goal should align with your vision for your life, with who you are, and be something that you are passionate about achieving. Passion and purpose are the fuel that ignites your persistence to arrive at your goal. If it's not something that you want in your heart, then you are not going to have much motivation to accomplish it.

_____
_____
_____
_____
_____
_____
_____
_____

WHY DO YOU BELIEVE THAT ACHIEVING THIS GOAL IS POSSIBLE AND REALISTIC FOR YOU?

You need to have confidence that reaching your goal is possible and realistic for *you*. If you don't, then you might end up sabotaging your own success.

_____

_____

_____

_____

_____

_____

_____

_____

_____

_____

WHAT'S YOUR WHY?

Why do you want to achieve this goal? Knowing your *why* is golden because it'll be the driving force of motivation and keep you going if times get tough. It'll help you discover a deep sense of purpose that you may have never realized you had and spark up your motivation! Write down the first thing that comes to mind.

_____

_____

Great job, lovely! Now let's dive deeper. Considering your answer above, ask yourself, "But why?" again. Do this several times until you've dug *really* deep down to an answer. This is where you'll find your core why. Let's get to digging...

NOW, WHAT'S YOUR CORE WHY?

"I'll write 100 first-draft pages of my self-help workbook."
Why? *"Because I've always wanted to write a book."*
Why? *"It would feel like a big accomplishment to write a book."*
Why? *"I would love to help people accomplish amazing breakthroughs that will uplift their lives."*
Why? *"I feel it's my mission to help others."*
But why...?

BUT WHY, LOVELY?

Dig Deep

_____

_____

_____

BUT WHY?

Dig Deeper

_____

_____

_____

KEEP DIGGING...

_____

_____

_____

_____

_____

_____

_____

_____

WHAT POSITIVE IMPACT WILL ACHIEVING YOUR GOAL HAVE ON YOUR LIFE AND OTHERS' LIVES?

_____

SECTION 3

Slaying Obstacles

"Don't give your obstacles superpowers."

—ROSEANNE BAKER

#GlamifyYourGoal

USE THE PAST TO YOUR ADVANTAGE

I'm going to warn you now, the path to accomplishing your goal isn't always going to be beautiful rainbows. There'll be days it will storm, and you might lack motivation, feel like giving up, or don't know how you are going to get through a big problem you're facing. If it was easy, then everyone would be doing it right? If you don't run into obstacles, you aren't stretching yourself enough girlfriend. Just know that this is normal and part of the process.

The best thing you can do is discover any potential obstacles now so that you can slay them and get your spectacular goal accomplished. Don't give your obstacles superpowers. Never allow your past "failures" to define your future or have power over your life. Instead choose to see them as learning experiences.

WHAT STOPPED YOU FROM ACHIEVING THIS GOAL OR OTHER GOALS IN THE PAST?

_____
_____
_____
_____
_____
_____
_____
_____

WHAT WILL IT TAKE TO MAKE SURE YOU ACHIEVE YOUR GOALS FROM THIS POINT FORWARD?

How can you learn from past experiences and use them to your advantage for future goals?

_____
_____
_____
_____
_____
_____
_____
_____
_____
_____
_____
_____

DISCOVER INTERNAL BLOCKS

Once you know what's stopping you from getting what you want, you can figure out how to get rid of it, take a detour around it, or face it directly and propel right through it with grace (as you are feeling the fear, anxiety, or negative feeling).

Take a few minutes to relax, close your eyes and vividly imagine the journey to achieving your goal. Really feel how it will feel. What feelings or thoughts do you have? Is there resistance, uncertainty, anxiety, or fears? Take some time to answer the questions below. The best thing you can do is be completely transparent with yourself. Your answers are where you'll find the secrets to unlocking hidden passageways that will lead to your success.

WHAT ARE SOME REASONS WHY YOU THINK THIS GOAL MIGHT NOT WORK?

"I don't have enough time. I'll have to work twice as hard."

1. _____
2. _____
3. _____
4. _____
5. _____

REWRITE THESE STATEMENTS AS POSITIVE SENTENCES

"I am willing to work twice as hard because it will be worth it."

1. _____
2. _____
3. _____
4. _____
5. _____

WHAT FEARS OR NEGATIVE BELIEFS DO YOU HAVE?

"I'm afraid that I might fail."

1. _____
2. _____
3. _____
4. _____
5. _____

REWRITE THESE STATEMENTS AS A POSITIVE SENTENCE

"I'm eager to do what it takes to succeed!"

1. _____
2. _____
3. _____
4. _____
5. _____

WHAT IS YOUR GREATEST INTERNAL OBSTACLE?

Where do you feel stuck?

___

HOW CAN YOU GET UNSTUCK?

___

WHAT WILL YOU GAIN BY ELIMINATING THIS OBSTACLE?

___

UNCOVER EXTERNAL OBSTACLES

WHAT OUTSIDE (EXTERNAL) RESOURCES ARE YOU LACKING?

This could be anything from money, skills, knowledge, mentors, etc.

"I don't know how to publish a book."

1. _____
2. _____
3. _____
4. _____
5. _____

HOW CAN YOU FIX THIS?

How can you solve these problems?

"I will call my friend who published a book and ask for guidance."

1. _____
2. _____
3. _____
4. _____
5. _____

WHAT IS YOUR GREATEST EXTERNAL OBSTACLE?

Where do you feel stuck?

_____
_____
_____
_____
_____
_____
_____
_____

HOW CAN YOU GET UNSTUCK?

_____
_____
_____
_____
_____
_____
_____

WHAT WILL YOU GAIN BY ELIMINATING THIS OBSTACLE?

_____
_____
_____
_____
_____

_____

_____

_____

So, how'd you do? Overcoming hurdles can be difficult, but it's one of the secrets to massive success. Affirm to yourself the following:

"I'm stronger than my greatest obstacle."

—ROSEANNE BAKER

#GlamifyYourGoal

YOUR DAZZLING RESOURCES

WHAT SKILLS, TALENTS, HABITS, OR QUALITIES DO YOU HAVE THAT WILL HELP YOU ACHIEVE YOUR GOAL?

_____

_____

_____

_____

_____

_____

LIST SOME POSITIVE PEOPLE YOU CAN SPEND TIME WITH WHO CAN HELP YOU ON YOUR GOAL-GETTING JOURNEY

You shouldn't try to achieve your goal alone (that's why I wrote this book for you ☺).

You need insight and help from others to achieve the quickest success — whether they provide emotional support, are your cheerleader, mentor, coach, a person you delegate tasks to, or an accountability partner. Only surround yourself with others who will uplift, encourage, and challenge you in a positive way.

WHO DO YOU KNOW WHO HAS ALREADY ACCOMPLISHED A GOAL SIMILAR TO YOURS?

This could be anyone—a mentor, coach, teacher, or friend. Who can you shadow, interview, or research at the library or online?

HOW DID THIS PERSON ACHIEVE THEIR GOAL?

What worked for them and what mistakes did they make so you won't do the same?

_____
_____
_____
_____
_____
_____
_____
_____

WHO CAN BE YOUR ACCOUNTABILITY PARTNER?

This is someone who will check in with you on a regular basis to make sure that you are staying on track with your goal and be available for any support you might need. It would help to find someone who is trying to achieve a similar goal. Contact this person now and write his or her name below.

My accountability partner is: _____

HOW OFTEN WILL THIS PERSON CHECK IN WITH YOU?

_____

WHAT WERE YOUR "AHA" MOMENTS IN THIS SECTION?

Moments of sudden realization, insight, or inspiration

_____
_____
_____
_____
_____
_____

SECTION 4

Get a Fabulous Mindset

"*Act as if you are fearless, and you will achieve things beyond your wildest imagination.*"

—ROSEANNE BAKER

#GlamifyYourGoal

CHANGE YOUR THINKING, CHANGE YOUR LIFE

Everything that you do or don't do is a direct result of what you believe about yourself. Beliefs are learned, which means that they can be unlearned. To determine what your beliefs are, ask yourself questions. Asking yourself questions can give you tons of insight into what your thought patterns are and how your thinking may be affecting your life. It's a good way to recognize any limits that you've placed on yourself so you can change the negative beliefs and stop them from blocking the way to your success.

WHY DO YOU BELIEVE YOU DESERVE TO ACHIEVE THIS GOAL?

WHAT IS YOUR DEFINITION OF SUCCESS?

_____
_____
_____
_____
_____
_____

WHY DO YOU BELIEVE THAT YOU ARE CAPABLE OF SUCCESSFULLY ACCOMPLISHING YOUR GOAL?

_____
_____
_____
_____
_____
_____

HOW CAN YOU ELIMINATE NEGATIVE BELIEFS YOU HAVE ABOUT YOUR ABILITY TO BE SUCCESSFUL?

_____
_____
_____
_____
_____
_____

THE MAGIC OF COMPLETE RESPONSIBILITY

When you are of the mindset that you have complete responsibility for your life, everything will change. Ok, I know the word "responsibility" might bring up negative feelings. Maybe it reminds you of a time when your parent yelled at you for not being responsible, or maybe you have some other negative association to the word. But when you have the mindset of "complete responsibility," you have a greater chance of being successful.

When you blame someone or something external (like another person or the economy) for the outcomes of situations, or for situations that you aren't pleased with, you are allowing yourself to believe you don't have control over your life.

When you believe that you are responsible for the quality of your life, you understand that you have the power to consciously shape your life—that you've got the magic wand, sweetie! Wonderful things begin to happen when you decide to take complete responsibility for your life.

One of the greatest days of your life is the day when you decide that your life is completely yours alone to steer in any direction that you want. This means that you can control your destiny and that there are no limits to what you can achieve. Awesome, right?!

WHAT CIRCUMSTANCES DO YOU TEND TO BLAME OTHER PEOPLE OR THINGS FOR?

Missing appointments.

When things don't go as planned.

_____
_____
_____
_____
_____
_____
_____
_____
_____
_____

WHEN THINGS DON'T HAPPEN THE WAY THAT YOU WANT, WHAT DO YOU TELL YOURSELF?

Are there excuses that you tend to make?

_____
_____
_____
_____
_____
_____
_____
_____
_____

HOW CAN YOU TAKE COMPLETE RESPONSIBILITY FOR YOUR LIFE STARTING NOW?

_____
_____
_____
_____
_____
_____
_____
_____
_____
_____
_____
_____
_____
_____
_____

N.O. MEANS NEXT OPPORTUNITY

You may have to get a "yes" from an outside source to achieve your goal—like getting hired with a company or having a manuscript accepted. One thing I want you to understand is if you get a "no" this does not mean that you failed. I believe it's a sign that a *better* opportunity is out there for you. Instead of seeing the word "no" as a signal of failure, I want you to think of it as *"next opportunity."* Always remember you are in control of making things happen. So, get out there with your awesome self and crush your goal gorgeous!

MINI VISION BOARD

When you constantly envision your goal as already having been achieved, the more real it will feel to you. A vision board can help you vividly see what it will be like when you reach your goal. It will be like a movie playing before you, showing what your life will be like once you hit your goal. I recommend that you view your vision board at least twice a day—first thing in the morning and just before going to bed each night.

When you are designing your board, I want you to think about things like:
- How will achieving your glamorous goal feel?
- What will your life look like?
- Who is with you?

You can fill your vision board with pictures, inspirational quotes, magazine clippings, drawings, or whatever your heart desires. There are no limits or judgments here. This is your vision, your goal, and ultimately your life. Have fun with this.

♦ Need inspiration for your vision board?
   Visit: http://www.breakthroughempire.com/glamifybonuses

AFFIRMATIONS FOR SUCCESS

Saying daily affirmations will help you program your mind for success and keep you in a positive mindset. Say them out loud and with conviction and feeling. Always begin the affirmation in the present tense (such as "I am…"), make sure that they are always positive statements, and keep them short.

WRITE YOUR AFFIRMATIONS IN THE HEARTS BELOW.

Write these affirmations on sticky notes and post them in places where you'll see them daily.

SECTION 5

Quitting is Not an Option

"There's always a solution - just allow yourself to be creative and you will discover it."

-ROSEANNE BAKER
#GlamifyYourGoal

EMERGENCY ACTION PLAN

If you ever feel like giving up, are experiencing low motivation, or having a big problem you don't know how to solve, visit this section. Always vow to be solution-oriented. You are never alone; you can always talk to a mentor, coach, or a friend.

My goal is _____	**HAVE A PROBLEM?**
Why I want this goal...	**The problem that I'm facing is...**
	Possible solutions are...(Psst, there's always a solution)
Achieving this goal will benefit my life and others' by...	*If my best friend were having this issue, I'd tell her...*
	What I can do now to resolve this is...
	I can use this experience to my advantage by...

IF I FEEL UNMOTIVATED, OR READY TO QUIT MY GOAL I'LL:

Take a walk, do something kind for someone, meditate, review my vision board, do yoga.

▼ As you achieve small or big wins on your path to success, write them down on a small piece of paper and keep them in a jar. When you are feeling down, you can pull one or as many as you wish out of the jar and read them to feel better quickly!

THE POWER OF JOY

Your thoughts create your reality and are more powerful than you might realize. Thoughts turn into feelings (good or bad), and your feelings turn into actions or inactions which ultimately create your reality. The great news is that you can literally change a bad thought or feeling into a good thought or feeling by surrounding yourself with images or thoughts of people, places, words, or things that lift your spirit.

Write down or draw everything you can think of that makes you feel joy. Refer to this page when you feel down, stressed, or want to feel more joy. You can include whatever you wish—this is your workbook, you know!

For more inspiration, check out your vision board on page 43.

SECTION 6

The Goal-Getter Plan

"Once you piece together the right steps in the correct order, your path to success will be golden."

-ROSEANNE BAKER

#GlamifyYourGoal

THE GOAL-GETTER PLAN

Yay, great job so far! You're approaching Day 1 of the ninety-day challenge. I bet you are excited to get started, but I want to give you a few tips before you begin. If you haven't completed the exercises in sections 1-4, please go back and do those first. Then come back to this section.

Before you start the challenge in the next section, you are going to build a solid action plan to achieve your goal. First, you will create a *Goal Mind Map*. Second, you'll design *The Success Blueprint*. Now let's figure out how to get you from where you are now to where you want to be!

GOAL MIND MAP

You need to determine every task that needs to be completed to arrive at your goal. A mind map will help you determine the milestones you'll need to take and then you'll break them into bite-sized action steps. Complete the *Goal Mind Map* on the next page.

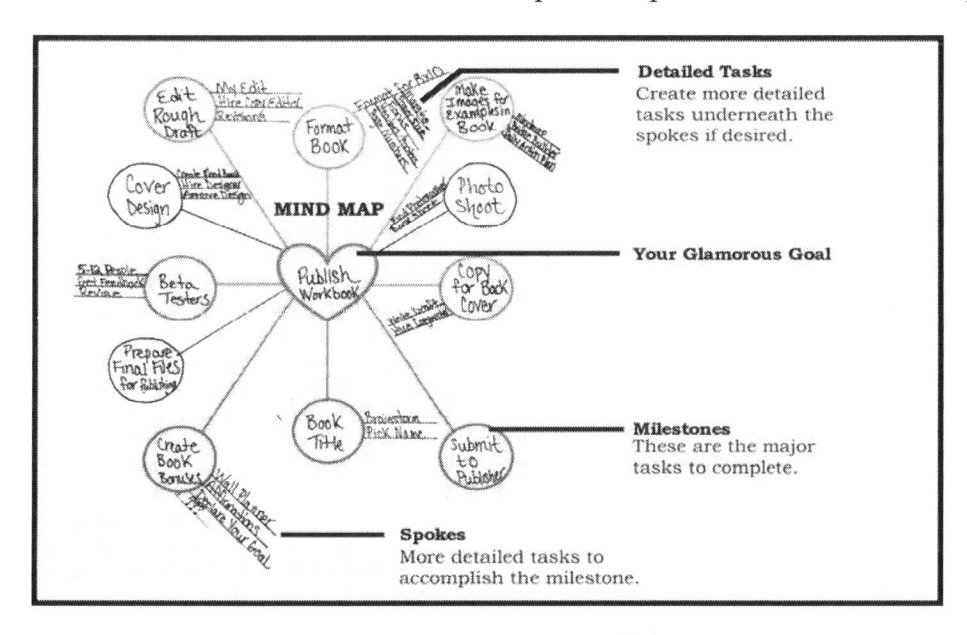

GLAMIFY YOUR GOAL

GOAL MIND MAP

THE SUCCESS BLUEPRINT

The path to achieve your goal isn't always clear. This exercise will help you create an aerial view of your plan so you always know what phase you are in and what tasks you should be working on. This will speed up your ability to take action because you already did the thinking.

Action 1: Write each milestone from the *Goal Mind Map* exercise (the tasks inside the circles), on separate flash cards or sticky notes. I recommend writing the tasks down on individual papers because you can rearrange them easily.

Action 2: Put the steps in order. Start with the last task first (the last step before achieving your goal) and work your way to the first task that you can start on now. The blueprint is not complete until each of the main branches is worked down to the initial steps (what tasks you can do right now).

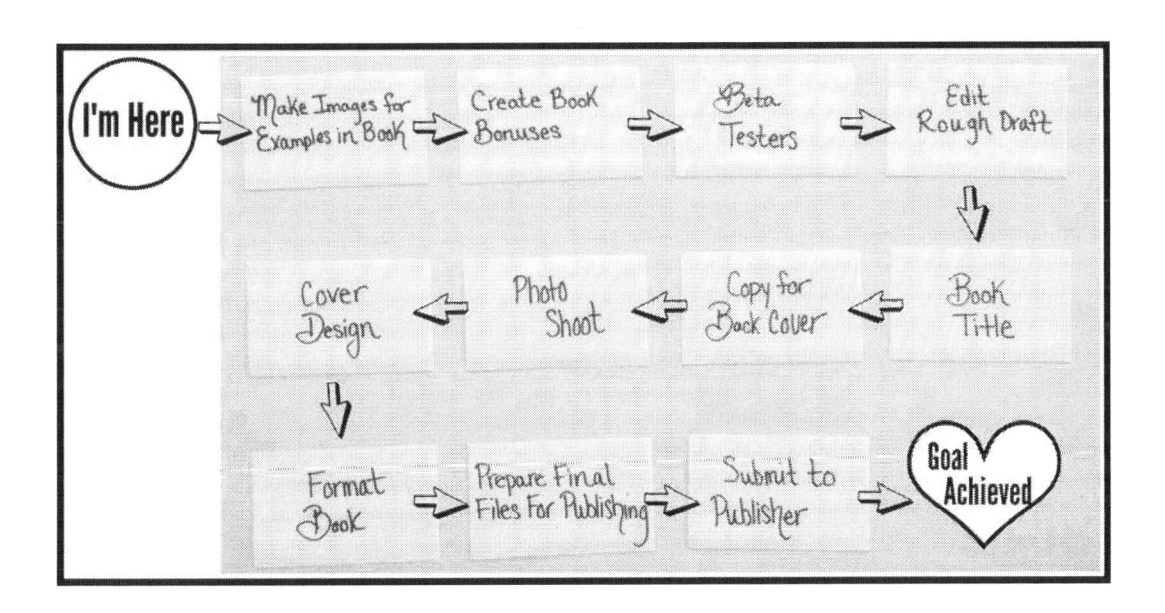

Action 3: Copy the order of tasks onto *The Success Blueprint* exercise. This way you'll have the action plan written down so you can refer to it throughout the challenge.

Action 4: Next to each milestone, write the estimated time frame needed to complete and the deadline.

Here's a sample of *The Success Blueprint*:

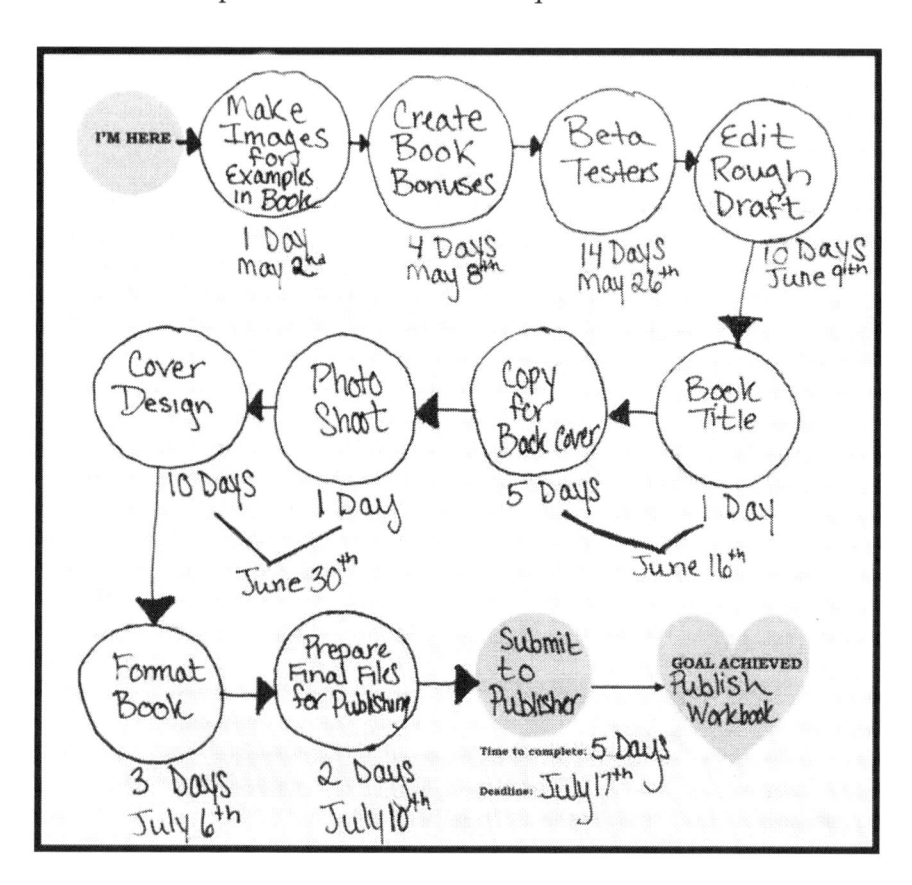

ROSEANNE BAKER

THE SUCCESS BLUEPRINT

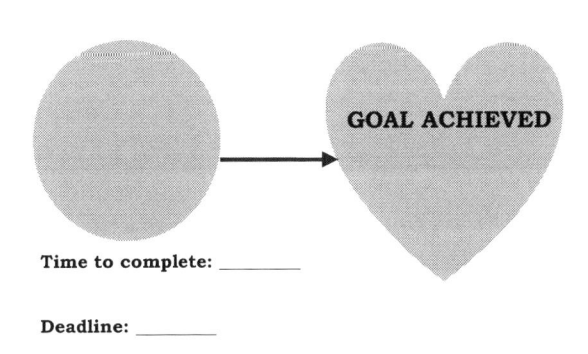

I'M HERE

GOAL ACHIEVED

Time to complete: _____

Deadline: _____

TIPS FOR PRODUCTIVITY, PLANNING, & SUCCESS

◆

5 TIPS TO SUPERCHARGE YOUR DAY
- Before stepping out of bed in the morning, think of three things you're grateful for
- Exercise
- Drink water
- Eat healthy
- View your vision board and imagine your goal as already being achieved

SCHEDULE THE MOST DIFFICULT TASKS FIRST THING IN THE MORNING
Once you take care of the harder tasks, you'll feel super motivated for the rest of the day and it'll be easier to get other items done.

SCHEDULE YOUR TIME IN BLOCKS
You'll get more done if you schedule tasks in *uninterrupted* time blocks of at least two hours. This means turn off your phone, email, have your spouse or a sitter watch the kids, etc. Hang up that do-not-disturb sign on the door and you'll be ready to conquer!

FINISH YOUR DAY FABULOUSLY
- Do the *End of Day Reflection* exercises on the *Daily Action Plan*
- Create your *Daily Action Plan* for the next day
- Look at your vision board again and visualize your goal
- Think about what you are grateful for

STAY CONSISTENT

Keep consistent for the *entire* challenge. Why? Because consistency will keep you motivated and on-track. You can definitely take a day off here and there and I encourage this to prevent burnout. Just be sure to make up for missed time on other days.

ACTION IS WHERE THE MAGIC IS

In order to make progress, you must take action. The more you work toward accomplishing your goal, the more transformation you will see. Planning is important but without action, your goal will remain a dream. And I know you don't want that!

TREAT YOURSELF LIKE YOU TREAT YOUR BEST FRIEND

You are embarking on a huge adventure, stepping outside your comfort zone and doing new things—so you'll likely face challenges along the way. It may be stressful and frustrating at times, but just know this is normal. Some days you may fall off-track or make mistakes. This is okay as long as you get right back on the path. Just know you'll be evolving and that this is a learning and growing experience.

REWARD YOURSELF

When you accomplish a mini round successfully, gift yourself something special. Decide what your reward will be at the beginning of each round and write it on the *Mini Goal Planner*. This will help keep you excited and supercharged and on the way to achieving your epic goal!

NEVER GIVE UP

There will be days when you want to quit and throw this book across the room! Please know that anything worth achieving isn't going to be easy. This workbook is here to help guide you when you're feeling stuck, down, or unmotivated. If you feel like giving up, tell your accountability partner, an encouraging friend, mentor, a family member, or check out the *Quitting is Not an Option Section* in this workbook on page 47.

SECTION 7

The Goal Planner

"The moment you take action, your dream begins to transform from just an idea to a visible reality."

—ROSEANNE BAKER

#GlamifyYourGoal

HOW TO USE THE PLANNER

HOW THE PLANNER IS DESIGNED

CREATE NINE MINI GOALS: Rather than thinking of your massive goal as one monster task to conquer, break it down to nine Mini Goals.

MINI GOAL PLANNER: Using the tasks from the *Goal Mind Map* on page 52 and the order of the steps from *The Success Blueprint* on page 55 you'll chunk your goal down into nine 10-day rounds. Each round will have a mini goal to achieve at the end. The idea is by the end of the ninety days, all of the mini goals you achieved will add up to achieving your big goal.

Each evening, refer to the *Mini Goal Planner* to see what tasks you can check off and what needs to be completed for the following day. You can also use the planner to make sure you are staying on track for the ninety-day deadline.

DAILY ACTION PLANNER: You have a daily action planner for each day of the challenge. It is best to fill out your action plan the evening before. Refer to your *Mini Goal Planner* to determine what items need to be worked on for that day.

Start with the top three things that *must* be done that day, preferably with the hardest task or the one you want to do least first. Then you can fill in any additional tasks if there is time and schedule any tasks that'll be delegated to others. If you have a regular daily planner, refer to it and see if you have any commitments already scheduled, and work around them. Don't forget to schedule time for resting, time with family and friends, and for doing activities you love. Each day will end with reflection questions so you can be conscious of your progress, identify any problems, and celebrate wins.

10-DAY REFLECTION: After each round, you will reflect on the previous ten days. You'll determine if you are on track to achieving your goal, discover what you need to do to get back on target if necessary, and acknowledge your accomplishments.

DECLARE YOUR GOAL

It's official—you have a written goal and action plan. You are ready to start the challenge, girl! Now, let's officially declare your *glamorous* goal.

Today I declare that I,

_____ will _____

(Your Name)　　　　　　　　　　(Your Glamorous Goal)

by _____

(Ninety-Day Deadline: Month/Day/Year)

x _____

(Your Fabulous Autograph)

" When you make your goal known publicly, you'll magnify your success. "

—ROSEANNE BAKER

#GlamifyYourGoal

Get a copy of this page to hang up on your wall at:
http://www.breakthroughempire.com/glamifybonuses

Now tell a mentor, friend, or an accountability partner what you've just declared. Take a picture of your declaration and send it to someone, mail it, or email it. This will help make you accountable and make your goal feel all the more real to you. If you don't want to share, that's ok, just declare it to yourself, love.

Are you ready to achieve your amazing goal? Turn the page because Day 1 of the challenge starts in 5...4...3...2...1...

SET YOUR MINI GOALS

WHAT ARE NINE MINI GOALS THAT YOU NEED TO ACHIEVE TO REACH YOUR EPIC GOAL?

There will be one mini goal for each of the nine rounds.

MINI GOAL

ROUND ONE: DAYS 1–10	
ROUND TWO: DAYS 11–20	
ROUND THREE: DAYS 21–30	
ROUND FOUR: DAYS 31–40	
ROUND FIVE: DAYS 41–50	
ROUND SIX: DAYS 51–60	
ROUND SEVEN: DAYS 61–70	
ROUND EIGHT: DAYS 71–80	
ROUND NINE: DAYS 81–90	

MINI GOAL PLANNER

ROUND ONE: DAYS 1-10

IF I SUCCESSFULLY COMPLETE THIS ROUND, I'LL REWARD MYSELF BY:
_____

♦ If a task has more than one action step, break the task down into smaller steps. This will help increase your focus and make it easier to take action.

MINI GOAL: _____

DATE: From _____ to _____

Done?	Tasks/Projects to Complete in Order of Sequence	Delegate Task To:
◊		
◊		
◊		
◊		
◊		
◊		
◊		
◊		
◊		
◊		
◊		
◊		
◊		
◊		

DAILY ACTION PLAN

DAY 1 OF 90

Date: _____

Morning Review

In 90-days I will: _____
My #1 focus today: _____
I'm grateful for: _____

SUCCESS LIST
3 THINGS I MUST DO TODAY
Do the least desired task first!

◇ _____

◇ _____

◇ _____

♦♦♦♦♦ OTHER TO-DO'S ♦♦♦♦♦
◇ _____
◇ _____
◇ _____
◇ _____

♦♦♦♦♦ TASKS TO DELEGATE ♦♦♦♦♦
◇ _____
◇ _____
◇ _____

♦♦♦♦♦ HABITS ♦♦♦♦♦
◇ Visualized My Goal
◇ Exercised
◇ 8 Glasses of Water
♡ ♡ ♡ ♡ ♡ ♡ ♡ ♡
◇ _____
◇ _____
◇ _____

SCHEDULE

4:00	
4:30	
5:00	
5:30	
6:00	
6:30	
7:00	
7:30	
8:00	
8:30	
9:00	
9:30	
10:00	
10:30	
11:00	
11:30	
12:00	
12:30	
1:00	
1:30	
2:00	
2:30	
3:00	
3:30	
4:00	
4:30	
5:00	
5:30	
6:00	
6:30	
7:00	
7:30	
8:00	
8:30	
9:00	
9:30	

End of Day Reflection:

What were your wins today?

What didn't happen & why? How can you fix this moving forward?

Great work today!

Schedule your action plan for tomorrow. →

My Brilliant Ideas or Notes

DAILY ACTION PLAN

DAY 2 OF 90

Date: _____

Morning Review

In 89-days I will: _____
My #1 focus today: _____
I'm grateful for: _____

SUCCESS LIST
3 THINGS I MUST DO TODAY
Do the least desired task first!

◊ _____

◊ _____

◊ _____

♦♦♦♦♦ OTHER TO-DO'S ♦♦♦♦♦
◊ _____
◊ _____
◊ _____
◊ _____

♦♦♦♦♦ TASKS TO DELEGATE ♦♦♦♦♦
◊ _____
◊ _____
◊ _____

♦♦♦♦♦ HABITS ♦♦♦♦♦
◊ Visualized My Goal
◊ Exercised
◊ 8 Glasses of Water
♡ ♡ ♡ ♡ ♡ ♡ ♡ ♡
◊ _____
◊ _____
◊ _____

SCHEDULE

4:00	
4:30	
5:00	
5:30	
6:00	
6:30	
7:00	
7:30	
8:00	
8:30	
9:00	
9:30	
10:00	
10:30	
11:00	
11:30	
12:00	
12:30	
1:00	
1:30	
2:00	
2:30	
3:00	
3:30	
4:00	
4:30	
5:00	
5:30	
6:00	
6:30	
7:00	
7:30	
8:00	
8:30	
9:00	
9:30	

End of Day Reflection:

What were your wins today?

What didn't happen & why? How can you fix this moving forward?

Great work today!

Schedule your action plan for tomorrow. →

My Brilliant Ideas or Notes

DAILY ACTION PLAN

DAY 3 OF 90

Date: _____

Morning Review

In 88-days I will: _____
My #1 focus today: _____
I'm grateful for: _____

SUCCESS LIST
3 THINGS I MUST DO TODAY
Do the least desired task first!

◊ _____

◊ _____

◊ _____

♦♦♦♦♦ OTHER TO-DO'S ♦♦♦♦♦
◊ _____
◊ _____
◊ _____
◊ _____

♦♦♦♦♦ TASKS TO DELEGATE ♦♦♦♦♦
◊ _____
◊ _____
◊ _____

♦♦♦♦♦ HABITS ♦♦♦♦♦
◊ Visualized My Goal
◊ Exercised
◊ 8 Glasses of Water
♡ ♡ ♡ ♡ ♡ ♡ ♡ ♡
◊ _____
◊ _____
◊ _____

SCHEDULE

4:00
4:30
5:00
5:30
6:00
6:30
7:00
7:30
8:00
8:30
9:00
9:30
10:00
10:30
11:00
11:30
12:00
12:30
1:00
1:30
2:00
2:30
3:00
3:30
4:00
4:30
5:00
5:30
6:00
6:30
7:00
7:30
8:00
8:30
9:00
9:30

End of Day Reflection:

What were your wins today?

What didn't happen & why? How can you fix this moving forward?

Great work today!

Schedule your action plan for tomorrow. →

My Brilliant Ideas or Notes

DAILY ACTION PLAN

DAY 4 OF 90

Date: _____

Morning Review

In 87-days I will: _____
My #1 focus today: _____
I'm grateful for: _____

SUCCESS LIST
3 THINGS I MUST DO TODAY
Do the least desired task first!

◊ _____

◊ _____

◊ _____

✦✦✦✦ OTHER TO-DO'S ✦✦✦✦

◊ _____
◊ _____
◊ _____
◊ _____

✦✦✦✦ TASKS TO DELEGATE ✦✦✦✦

◊ _____
◊ _____
◊ _____

✦✦✦✦ HABITS ✦✦✦✦
◊ Visualized My Goal
◊ Exercised
◊ 8 Glasses of Water
♡ ♡ ♡ ♡ ♡ ♡ ♡ ♡

◊ _____
◊ _____
◊ _____

SCHEDULE

4:00	
4:30	
5:00	
5:30	
6:00	
6:30	
7:00	
7:30	
8:00	
8:30	
9:00	
9:30	
10:00	
10:30	
11:00	
11:30	
12:00	
12:30	
1:00	
1:30	
2:00	
2:30	
3:00	
3:30	
4:00	
4:30	
5:00	
5:30	
6:00	
6:30	
7:00	
7:30	
8:00	
8:30	
9:00	
9:30	

End of Day Reflection:

What were your wins today?

What didn't happen & why? How can you fix this moving forward?

Great work today!

Schedule your action plan for tomorrow. →

My Brilliant Ideas or Notes

DAILY ACTION PLAN

DAY 5 OF 90

Date: _____

Morning Review

In 86-days I will: _____
My #1 focus today: _____
I'm grateful for: _____

SUCCESS LIST
3 THINGS I MUST DO TODAY
Do the least desired task first!

◊ _____

◊ _____

◊ _____

♦♦♦♦♦ OTHER TO-DO'S ♦♦♦♦♦

◊ _____
◊ _____
◊ _____
◊ _____

♦♦♦♦♦ TASKS TO DELEGATE ♦♦♦♦♦

◊ _____
◊ _____
◊ _____

♦♦♦♦♦ HABITS ♦♦♦♦♦

◊ Visualized My Goal
◊ Exercised
◊ 8 Glasses of Water

♡ ♡ ♡ ♡ ♡ ♡ ♡ ♡

◊ _____
◊ _____
◊ _____

SCHEDULE

4:00
4:30
5:00
5:30
6:00
6:30
7:00
7:30
8:00
8:30
9:00
9:30
10:00
10:30
11:00
11:30
12:00
12:30
1:00
1:30
2:00
2:30
3:00
3:30
4:00
4:30
5:00
5:30
6:00
6:30
7:00
7:30
8:00
8:30
9:00
9:30

End of Day Reflection:

What were your wins today?

What didn't happen & why? How can you fix this moving forward?

Great work today!

Schedule your action plan for tomorrow. →

My Brilliant Ideas or Notes

DAILY ACTION PLAN

DAY 6 OF 90

Date: _____

Morning Review

In 85-days I will: _____
My #1 focus today: _____
I'm grateful for: _____

SUCCESS LIST
3 THINGS I MUST DO TODAY
Do the least desired task first!

◇ _____

◇ _____

◇ _____

♦♦♦♦ OTHER TO-DO'S ♦♦♦♦
◇ _____
◇ _____
◇ _____
◇ _____

♦♦♦♦ TASKS TO DELEGATE ♦♦♦♦
◇ _____
◇ _____
◇ _____

♦♦♦ HABITS ♦♦♦
◇ Visualized My Goal
◇ Exercised
◇ 8 Glasses of Water
♡ ♡ ♡ ♡ ♡ ♡ ♡ ♡
◇ _____
◇ _____
◇ _____

SCHEDULE

4:00	
4:30	
5:00	
5:30	
6:00	
6:30	
7:00	
7:30	
8:00	
8:30	
9:00	
9:30	
10:00	
10:30	
11:00	
11:30	
12:00	
12:30	
1:00	
1:30	
2:00	
2:30	
3:00	
3:30	
4:00	
4:30	
5:00	
5:30	
6:00	
6:30	
7:00	
7:30	
8:00	
8:30	
9:00	
9:30	

End of Day Reflection:

What were your wins today?

What didn't happen & why? How can you fix this moving forward?

Great work today!

Schedule your action plan for tomorrow. →

My Brilliant Ideas or Notes

DAILY ACTION PLAN

DAY 7 OF 90
Date: _____

Morning Review

In 84-days I will: _____
My #1 focus today: _____
I'm grateful for: _____

SUCCESS LIST
3 THINGS I MUST DO TODAY
Do the least desired task first!

◇ _____

◇ _____

◇ _____

♦♦♦♦♦ OTHER TO-DO'S ♦♦♦♦♦
◇ _____
◇ _____
◇ _____
◇ _____

♦♦♦♦♦ TASKS TO DELEGATE ♦♦♦♦♦
◇ _____
◇ _____
◇ _____

♦♦♦♦♦ HABITS ♦♦♦♦♦
◇ Visualized My Goal
◇ Exercised
◇ 8 Glasses of Water
♡ ♡ ♡ ♡ ♡ ♡ ♡ ♡
◇ _____
◇ _____
◇ _____

SCHEDULE

4:00	
4:30	
5:00	
5:30	
6:00	
6:30	
7:00	
7:30	
8:00	
8:30	
9:00	
9:30	
10:00	
10:30	
11:00	
11:30	
12:00	
12:30	
1:00	
1:30	
2:00	
2:30	
3:00	
3:30	
4:00	
4:30	
5:00	
5:30	
6:00	
6:30	
7:00	
7:30	
8:00	
8:30	
9:00	
9:30	

End of Day Reflection:

What were your wins today?

What didn't happen & why? How can you fix this moving forward?

Great work today!

Schedule your action plan for tomorrow. →

My Brilliant Ideas or Notes

DAILY ACTION PLAN

DAY 8 OF 90
Date: _____

Morning Review

In 83-days I will: _____
My #1 focus today: _____
I'm grateful for: _____

SUCCESS LIST
3 THINGS I MUST DO TODAY
Do the least desired task first!

◊ _____

◊ _____

◊ _____

✦✦✦✦ OTHER TO-DO'S ✦✦✦✦

◊ _____
◊ _____
◊ _____
◊ _____

✦✦✦✦ TASKS TO DELEGATE ✦✦✦✦

◊ _____
◊ _____
◊ _____

✦✦✦ HABITS ✦✦✦

◊ Visualized My Goal
◊ Exercised
◊ 8 Glasses of Water
♡ ♡ ♡ ♡ ♡ ♡ ♡ ♡

◊ _____
◊ _____
◊ _____

SCHEDULE

4:00
4:30
5:00
5:30
6:00
6:30
7:00
7:30
8:00
8:30
9:00
9:30
10:00
10:30
11:00
11:30
12:00
12:30
1:00
1:30
2:00
2:30
3:00
3:30
4:00
4:30
5:00
5:30
6:00
6:30
7:00
7:30
8:00
8:30
9:00
9:30

End of Day Reflection:

What were your wins today?

What didn't happen & why? How can you fix this moving forward?

Great work today!

Schedule your action plan for tomorrow. →

My Brilliant Ideas or Notes

DAILY ACTION PLAN

DAY 9 OF 90

Date: _____

Morning Review

In 82-days I will: _____
My #1 focus today: _____
I'm grateful for: _____

SUCCESS LIST
3 THINGS I MUST DO TODAY
Do the least desired task first!

◊ _____

◊ _____

◊ _____

♦♦♦♦♦ OTHER TO-DO'S ♦♦♦♦♦
◊ _____
◊ _____
◊ _____
◊ _____

♦♦♦♦♦ TASKS TO DELEGATE ♦♦♦♦♦
◊ _____
◊ _____
◊ _____

♦♦♦♦♦ HABITS ♦♦♦♦♦
◊ Visualized My Goal
◊ Exercised
◊ 8 Glasses of Water
♡ ♡ ♡ ♡ ♡ ♡ ♡ ♡
◊ _____
◊ _____
◊ _____

SCHEDULE
4:00	
4:30	
5:00	
5:30	
6:00	
6:30	
7:00	
7:30	
8:00	
8:30	
9:00	
9:30	
10:00	
10:30	
11:00	
11:30	
12:00	
12:30	
1:00	
1:30	
2:00	
2:30	
3:00	
3:30	
4:00	
4:30	
5:00	
5:30	
6:00	
6:30	
7:00	
7:30	
8:00	
8:30	
9:00	
9:30	

End of Day Reflection:

What were your wins today?

What didn't happen & why? How can you fix this moving forward?

Great work today!

Schedule your action plan for tomorrow. →

My Brilliant Ideas or Notes

DAILY ACTION PLAN

DAY 10 OF 90

Date: _____

Morning Review

In 81-days I will: _____
My #1 focus today: _____
I'm grateful for: _____

SUCCESS LIST
3 THINGS I MUST DO TODAY
Do the least desired task first!

◊ _____

◊ _____

◊ _____

♦♦♦♦ OTHER TO-DO'S ♦♦♦♦
◊ _____
◊ _____
◊ _____
◊ _____

♦♦♦♦ TASKS TO DELEGATE ♦♦♦♦
◊ _____
◊ _____
◊ _____

♦♦♦♦ HABITS ♦♦♦♦
◊ Visualized My Goal
◊ Exercised
◊ 8 Glasses of Water
♡ ♡ ♡ ♡ ♡ ♡ ♡ ♡
◊ _____
◊ _____
◊ _____

SCHEDULE
4:00	
4:30	
5:00	
5:30	
6:00	
6:30	
7:00	
7:30	
8:00	
8:30	
9:00	
9:30	
10:00	
10:30	
11:00	
11:30	
12:00	
12:30	
1:00	
1:30	
2:00	
2:30	
3:00	
3:30	
4:00	
4:30	
5:00	
5:30	
6:00	
6:30	
7:00	
7:30	
8:00	
8:30	
9:00	
9:30	

End of Day Reflection:

What were your wins today?

What didn't happen & why? How can you fix this moving forward?

Great work today!

Schedule your action plan for tomorrow. →

My Brilliant Ideas or Notes

ROUND ONE: REFLECTION

DID YOU ACHIEVE YOUR MINI GOAL THIS ROUND?
Don't forget to reward yourself!

WHAT SURPRISE ACCOMPLISHMENT DID YOU ACHIEVE?

WHAT DIDN'T HAPPEN OR GO AS PLANNED?

HOW CAN YOU FIX THIS SO IT DOESN'T HAPPEN IN THE FUTURE?

WHAT WAS THE MOST VALUABLE LESSON YOU LEARNED?

ARE YOU ON TRACK TO ACCOMPLISHING YOUR GOAL?
IF NOT, WHAT CAN YOU DO TO FIX THIS?

Delegate items or find a way to free up more time.

_____
_____
_____
_____
_____

IS ANYTHING LEFT UNFINISHED?
IF SO, HOW DO YOU PLAN TO COMPLETE IT?

_____
_____
_____
_____
_____

WHAT ARE YOU MOST GRATEFUL FOR?

_____
_____
_____
_____
_____

Great job this round girl! Now let's plan Round Two. →

MINI GOAL PLANNER

ROUND TWO: DAYS 11–20

IF I SUCCESSFULLY COMPLETE THIS ROUND, I'LL REWARD MYSELF BY:

_____

♦ If a task has more than one action step, break the task down into smaller steps. This will help increase your focus and make it easier to take action.

MINI GOAL: _____

DATE: From _____ to _____

Done?	Tasks/Projects to Complete in Order of Sequence	Delegate Task To:
◊		
◊		
◊		
◊		
◊		
◊		
◊		
◊		
◊		
◊		
◊		
◊		
◊		
◊		

DAILY ACTION PLAN

DAY 11 OF 90
Date: _____

Morning Review

In 80-days I will: _____
My #1 focus today: _____
I'm grateful for: _____

SUCCESS LIST
3 THINGS I MUST DO TODAY
Do the least desired task first!

◇ _____

◇ _____

◇ _____

✦✦✦✦ OTHER TO-DO'S ✦✦✦✦

◇ _____
◇ _____
◇ _____
◇ _____

✦✦✦✦ TASKS TO DELEGATE ✦✦✦✦

◇ _____
◇ _____
◇ _____

✦✦✦ HABITS ✦✦✦

◇ Visualized My Goal
◇ Exercised
◇ 8 Glasses of Water
♡ ♡ ♡ ♡ ♡ ♡ ♡ ♡

◇ _____
◇ _____
◇ _____

SCHEDULE

4:00	
4:30	
5:00	
5:30	
6:00	
6:30	
7:00	
7:30	
8:00	
8:30	
9:00	
9:30	
10:00	
10:30	
11:00	
11:30	
12:00	
12:30	
1:00	
1:30	
2:00	
2:30	
3:00	
3:30	
4:00	
4:30	
5:00	
5:30	
6:00	
6:30	
7:00	
7:30	
8:00	
8:30	
9:00	
9:30	

End of Day Reflection:

What were your wins today?

What didn't happen & why? How can you fix this moving forward?

Great work today!

Schedule your action plan for tomorrow. →

My Brilliant Ideas or Notes

DAILY ACTION PLAN

DAY 12 OF 90

Date: _____

Morning Review

In 79-days I will: _____
My #1 focus today: _____
I'm grateful for: _____

SUCCESS LIST
3 THINGS I MUST DO TODAY
Do the least desired task first!

◇ _____

◇ _____

◇ _____

♦♦♦♦♦ OTHER TO-DO'S ♦♦♦♦♦
◇ _____
◇ _____
◇ _____
◇ _____

♦♦♦♦♦ TASKS TO DELEGATE ♦♦♦♦♦
◇ _____
◇ _____
◇ _____

♦♦♦♦♦ HABITS ♦♦♦♦♦
◇ Visualized My Goal
◇ Exercised
◇ 8 Glasses of Water
♡ ♡ ♡ ♡ ♡ ♡ ♡ ♡
◇ _____
◇ _____
◇ _____

SCHEDULE

4:00	
4:30	
5:00	
5:30	
6:00	
6:30	
7:00	
7:30	
8:00	
8:30	
9:00	
9:30	
10:00	
10:30	
11:00	
11:30	
12:00	
12:30	
1:00	
1:30	
2:00	
2:30	
3:00	
3:30	
4:00	
4:30	
5:00	
5:30	
6:00	
6:30	
7:00	
7:30	
8:00	
8:30	
9:00	
9:30	

End of Day Reflection:

What were your wins today?

What didn't happen & why? How can you fix this moving forward?

Great work today!

Schedule your action plan for tomorrow. →

My Brilliant Ideas or Notes

DAILY ACTION PLAN

DAY 13 OF 90
Date: _____

Morning Review

In 78-days I will: _____
My #1 focus today: _____
I'm grateful for: _____

SUCCESS LIST
3 THINGS I MUST DO TODAY
Do the least desired task first!

◊ _____

◊ _____

◊ _____

◆◆◆◆◆ OTHER TO-DO'S ◆◆◆◆◆
◊ _____
◊ _____
◊ _____
◊ _____

◆◆◆◆◆ TASKS TO DELEGATE ◆◆◆◆◆
◊ _____
◊ _____
◊ _____

◆◆◆◆◆ HABITS ◆◆◆◆◆
◊ Visualized My Goal
◊ Exercised
◊ 8 Glasses of Water
♡ ♡ ♡ ♡ ♡ ♡ ♡ ♡
◊ _____
◊ _____
◊ _____

SCHEDULE

4:00	
4:30	
5:00	
5:30	
6:00	
6:30	
7:00	
7:30	
8:00	
8:30	
9:00	
9:30	
10:00	
10:30	
11:00	
11:30	
12:00	
12:30	
1:00	
1:30	
2:00	
2:30	
3:00	
3:30	
4:00	
4:30	
5:00	
5:30	
6:00	
6:30	
7:00	
7:30	
8:00	
8:30	
9:00	
9:30	

End of Day Reflection:

What were your wins today?

What didn't happen & why? How can you fix this moving forward?

Great work today!

Schedule your action plan for tomorrow. →

My Brilliant Ideas or Notes

DAILY ACTION PLAN

DAY 14 OF 90
Date: _____

Morning Review

In 77-days I will: _____
My #1 focus today: _____
I'm grateful for: _____

SUCCESS LIST
3 THINGS I MUST DO TODAY
Do the least desired task first!

◊ _____

◊ _____

◊ _____

♦♦♦♦♦ OTHER TO-DO'S ♦♦♦♦♦
◊ _____
◊ _____
◊ _____
◊ _____

♦♦♦♦♦ TASKS TO DELEGATE ♦♦♦♦♦
◊ _____
◊ _____
◊ _____

♦♦♦♦♦ HABITS ♦♦♦♦♦
◊ Visualized My Goal
◊ Exercised
◊ 8 Glasses of Water
♡ ♡ ♡ ♡ ♡ ♡ ♡ ♡
◊ _____
◊ _____
◊ _____

SCHEDULE

4:00	
4:30	
5:00	
5:30	
6:00	
6:30	
7:00	
7:30	
8:00	
8:30	
9:00	
9:30	
10:00	
10:30	
11:00	
11:30	
12:00	
12:30	
1:00	
1:30	
2:00	
2:30	
3:00	
3:30	
4:00	
4:30	
5:00	
5:30	
6:00	
6:30	
7:00	
7:30	
8:00	
8:30	
9:00	
9:30	

End of Day Reflection:

What were your wins today?

What didn't happen & why? How can you fix this moving forward?

Great work today!

Schedule your action plan for tomorrow. →

My Brilliant Ideas or Notes

DAILY ACTION PLAN

DAY 15 OF 90
Date: _____

Morning Review

In 76-days I will: _____
My #1 focus today: _____
I'm grateful for: _____

SUCCESS LIST
3 THINGS I MUST DO TODAY
Do the least desired task first!

◊ _____

◊ _____

◊ _____

✦✦✦✦ OTHER TO-DO'S ✦✦✦✦
◊ _____
◊ _____
◊ _____
◊ _____

✦✦✦✦ TASKS TO DELEGATE ✦✦✦✦
◊ _____
◊ _____
◊ _____

✦✦✦ HABITS ✦✦✦
◊ Visualized My Goal
◊ Exercised
◊ 8 Glasses of Water
♡ ♡ ♡ ♡ ♡ ♡ ♡ ♡

◊ _____
◊ _____
◊ _____

SCHEDULE

4:00	
4:30	
5:00	
5:30	
6:00	
6:30	
7:00	
7:30	
8:00	
8:30	
9:00	
9:30	
10:00	
10:30	
11:00	
11:30	
12:00	
12:30	
1:00	
1:30	
2:00	
2:30	
3:00	
3:30	
4:00	
4:30	
5:00	
5:30	
6:00	
6:30	
7:00	
7:30	
8:00	
8:30	
9:00	
9:30	

End of Day Reflection:

What were your wins today?

What didn't happen & why? How can you fix this moving forward?

Great work today!

Schedule your action plan for tomorrow. →

My Brilliant Ideas or Notes

DAILY ACTION PLAN

DAY 16 OF 90
Date: _____

Morning Review

In 75-days I will: _____
My #1 focus today: _____
I'm grateful for: _____

SUCCESS LIST
3 THINGS I MUST DO TODAY
Do the least desired task first!

◊ _____

◊ _____

◊ _____

♦♦♦♦♦ OTHER TO-DO'S ♦♦♦♦♦
◊ _____
◊ _____
◊ _____
◊ _____

♦♦♦♦♦ TASKS TO DELEGATE ♦♦♦♦♦
◊ _____
◊ _____
◊ _____

♦♦♦♦♦ HABITS ♦♦♦♦♦
◊ Visualized My Goal
◊ Exercised
◊ 8 Glasses of Water
♡ ♡ ♡ ♡ ♡
◊ _____
◊ _____
◊ _____

SCHEDULE

4:00	
4:30	
5:00	
5:30	
6:00	
6:30	
7:00	
7:30	
8:00	
8:30	
9:00	
9:30	
10:00	
10:30	
11:00	
11:30	
12:00	
12:30	
1:00	
1:30	
2:00	
2:30	
3:00	
3:30	
4:00	
4:30	
5:00	
5:30	
6:00	
6:30	
7:00	
7:30	
8:00	
8:30	
9:00	
9:30	

End of Day Reflection:

What were your wins today?

What didn't happen & why? How can you fix this moving forward?

Great work today!

Schedule your action plan for tomorrow. →

My Brilliant Ideas or Notes

DAILY ACTION PLAN

DAY 17 OF 90

Date: _____

Morning Review

In 74-days I will: _____
My #1 focus today: _____
I'm grateful for: _____

SUCCESS LIST
3 THINGS I MUST DO TODAY
Do the least desired task first!

◊ _____
◊ _____
◊ _____

✦✦✦✦ OTHER TO-DO'S ✦✦✦✦
◊ _____
◊ _____
◊ _____
◊ _____

✦✦✦✦ TASKS TO DELEGATE ✦✦✦✦
◊ _____
◊ _____
◊ _____

✦✦✦✦ HABITS ✦✦✦✦
◊ Visualized My Goal
◊ Exercised
◊ 8 Glasses of Water
♡ ♡ ♡ ♡ ♡ ♡ ♡ ♡
◊ _____
◊ _____
◊ _____

SCHEDULE
4:00
4:30
5:00
5:30
6:00
6:30
7:00
7:30
8:00
8:30
9:00
9:30
10:00
10:30
11:00
11:30
12:00
12:30
1:00
1:30
2:00
2:30
3:00
3:30
4:00
4:30
5:00
5:30
6:00
6:30
7:00
7:30
8:00
8:30
9:00
9:30

End of Day Reflection:

What were your wins today?

What didn't happen & why? How can you fix this moving forward?

Great work today!

Schedule your action plan for tomorrow. →

My Brilliant Ideas or Notes

DAILY ACTION PLAN

DAY 18 OF 90

Date: _____

Morning Review

In 73-days I will: _____
My #1 focus today: _____
I'm grateful for: _____

SUCCESS LIST
3 THINGS I MUST DO TODAY
Do the least desired task first!

◊ _____

◊ _____

◊ _____

♦♦♦♦♦ OTHER TO-DO'S ♦♦♦♦♦

◊ _____
◊ _____
◊ _____
◊ _____

♦♦♦♦♦ TASKS TO DELEGATE ♦♦♦♦♦

◊ _____
◊ _____
◊ _____

♦♦♦♦♦ HABITS ♦♦♦♦♦

◊ Visualized My Goal
◊ Exercised
◊ 8 Glasses of Water
♡♡♡♡♡♡♡♡
◊ _____
◊ _____
◊ _____

SCHEDULE

4:00
4:30
5:00
5:30
6:00
6:30
7:00
7:30
8:00
8:30
9:00
9:30
10:00
10:30
11:00
11:30
12:00
12:30
1:00
1:30
2:00
2:30
3:00
3:30
4:00
4:30
5:00
5:30
6:00
6:30
7:00
7:30
8:00
8:30
9:00
9:30

End of Day Reflection:

What were your wins today?

What didn't happen & why? How can you fix this moving forward?

Great work today!

Schedule your action plan for tomorrow. →

My Brilliant Ideas or Notes

DAILY ACTION PLAN

DAY 19 OF 90

Date: _____

Morning Review

In 72-days I will: _____
My #1 focus today: _____
I'm grateful for: _____

SUCCESS LIST
3 THINGS I MUST DO TODAY
Do the least desired task first!

◇ _____

◇ _____

◇ _____

◆◆◆◆◆ OTHER TO-DO'S ◆◆◆◆◆
◇ _____
◇ _____
◇ _____
◇ _____

◆◆◆◆◆ TASKS TO DELEGATE ◆◆◆◆◆
◇ _____
◇ _____
◇ _____

◆◆◆◆◆ HABITS ◆◆◆◆◆
◇ Visualized My Goal
◇ Exercised
◇ 8 Glasses of Water
♡ ♡ ♡ ♡ ♡ ♡ ♡ ♡
◇ _____
◇ _____
◇ _____

SCHEDULE

4:00	
4:30	
5:00	
5:30	
6:00	
6:30	
7:00	
7:30	
8:00	
8:30	
9:00	
9:30	
10:00	
10:30	
11:00	
11:30	
12:00	
12:30	
1:00	
1:30	
2:00	
2:30	
3:00	
3:30	
4:00	
4:30	
5:00	
5:30	
6:00	
6:30	
7:00	
7:30	
8:00	
8:30	
9:00	
9:30	

End of Day Reflection:

What were your wins today?

What didn't happen & why? How can you fix this moving forward?

Great work today!

Schedule your action plan for tomorrow. →

My Brilliant Ideas or Notes

DAILY ACTION PLAN

DAY 20 OF 90
Date: _____

Morning Review

In 71-days I will: _____
My #1 focus today: _____
I'm grateful for: _____

SUCCESS LIST
3 THINGS I MUST DO TODAY
Do the least desired task first!

◊ _____

◊ _____

◊ _____

♦♦♦♦ OTHER TO-DO'S ♦♦♦♦
◊ _____
◊ _____
◊ _____
◊ _____

♦♦♦♦ TASKS TO DELEGATE ♦♦♦♦
◊ _____
◊ _____
◊ _____

♦♦♦♦ HABITS ♦♦♦♦
◊ Visualized My Goal
◊ Exercised
◊ 8 Glasses of Water
♡ ♡ ♡ ♡ ♡ ♡ ♡ ♡
◊ _____
◊ _____
◊ _____

SCHEDULE

4:00	
4:30	
5:00	
5:30	
6:00	
6:30	
7:00	
7:30	
8:00	
8:30	
9:00	
9:30	
10:00	
10:30	
11:00	
11:30	
12:00	
12:30	
1:00	
1:30	
2:00	
2:30	
3:00	
3:30	
4:00	
4:30	
5:00	
5:30	
6:00	
6:30	
7:00	
7:30	
8:00	
8:30	
9:00	
9:30	

End of Day Reflection:

What were your wins today?

What didn't happen & why? How can you fix this moving forward?

Great work today!

Schedule your action plan for tomorrow. →

My Brilliant Ideas or Notes

ROUND TWO: REFLECTION

DID YOU ACHIEVE YOUR MINI GOAL THIS ROUND?

Don't forget to reward yourself!

_____

WHAT SURPRISE ACCOMPLISHMENT DID YOU ACHIEVE?

_____
_____

WHAT DIDN'T HAPPEN OR GO AS PLANNED?

_____
_____
_____

HOW CAN YOU FIX THIS SO IT DOESN'T HAPPEN IN THE FUTURE?

_____
_____
_____

WHAT WAS THE MOST VALUABLE LESSON YOU LEARNED?

_____
_____

ARE YOU ON TRACK TO ACCOMPLISHING YOUR GOAL?
IF NOT, WHAT CAN YOU DO TO FIX THIS?

Delegate items or find a way to free up more time.

_____
_____
_____
_____
_____

IS ANYTHING LEFT UNFINISHED?
IF SO, HOW DO YOU PLAN TO COMPLETE IT?

_____
_____
_____
_____
_____

WHAT ARE YOU MOST GRATEFUL FOR?

_____
_____
_____
_____
_____

Great job this round girl! Now let's plan Round Three. →

MINI GOAL PLANNER

ROUND THREE: DAYS 21-30

IF I SUCCESSFULLY COMPLETE THIS ROUND, I'LL REWARD MYSELF BY:
_____

♦ If a task has more than one action step, break the task down into smaller steps. This will help increase your focus and make it easier to take action.

MINI GOAL: _____

DATE: From _____ **to** _____

Done?	Tasks/Projects to Complete in Order of Sequence	Delegate Task To:
◊		
◊		
◊		
◊		
◊		
◊		
◊		
◊		
◊		
◊		
◊		
◊		
◊		
◊		

DAILY ACTION PLAN

DAY 21 OF 90

Date: _____

Morning Review

In 70-days I will: _____
My #1 focus today: _____
I'm grateful for: _____

SUCCESS LIST
3 THINGS I MUST DO TODAY
Do the least desired task first!

◊ _____

◊ _____

◊ _____

✦✦✦✦✦ OTHER TO-DO'S ✦✦✦✦✦
◊ _____
◊ _____
◊ _____
◊ _____

✦✦✦✦✦ TASKS TO DELEGATE ✦✦✦✦✦
◊ _____
◊ _____
◊ _____

✦✦✦✦✦ HABITS ✦✦✦✦✦
◊ Visualized My Goal
◊ Exercised
◊ 8 Glasses of Water
♡ ♡ ♡ ♡ ♡ ♡ ♡ ♡
◊ _____
◊ _____
◊ _____

SCHEDULE

4:00	
4:30	
5:00	
5:30	
6:00	
6:30	
7:00	
7:30	
8:00	
8:30	
9:00	
9:30	
10:00	
10:30	
11:00	
11:30	
12:00	
12:30	
1:00	
1:30	
2:00	
2:30	
3:00	
3:30	
4:00	
4:30	
5:00	
5:30	
6:00	
6:30	
7:00	
7:30	
8:00	
8:30	
9:00	
9:30	

End of Day Reflection:

What were your wins today?

What didn't happen & why? How can you fix this moving forward?

Great work today!

Schedule your action plan for tomorrow. →

My Brilliant Ideas or Notes

DAILY ACTION PLAN

DAY 22 OF 90

Date: _____

Morning Review

In 69-days I will: _____
My #1 focus today: _____
I'm grateful for: _____

SUCCESS LIST
3 THINGS I MUST DO TODAY
Do the least desired task first!

◊ _____

◊ _____

◊ _____

♦♦♦♦♦ OTHER TO-DO'S ♦♦♦♦♦
◊ _____
◊ _____
◊ _____
◊ _____

♦♦♦♦♦ TASKS TO DELEGATE ♦♦♦♦♦
◊ _____
◊ _____
◊ _____

♦♦♦♦♦ HABITS ♦♦♦♦♦
◊ Visualized My Goal
◊ Exercised
◊ 8 Glasses of Water
♡ ♡ ♡ ♡ ♡ ♡ ♡ ♡
◊ _____
◊ _____
◊ _____

SCHEDULE

4:00	
4:30	
5:00	
5:30	
6:00	
6:30	
7:00	
7:30	
8:00	
8:30	
9:00	
9:30	
10:00	
10:30	
11:00	
11:30	
12:00	
12:30	
1:00	
1:30	
2:00	
2:30	
3:00	
3:30	
4:00	
4:30	
5:00	
5:30	
6:00	
6:30	
7:00	
7:30	
8:00	
8:30	
9:00	
9:30	

End of Day Reflection:

What were your wins today?

What didn't happen & why? How can you fix this moving forward?

Great work today!

Schedule your action plan for tomorrow. →

My Brilliant Ideas or Notes

DAILY ACTION PLAN

DAY 23 OF 90

Date: _____

Morning Review

In 68-days I will: _____
My #1 focus today: _____
I'm grateful for: _____

SUCCESS LIST
3 THINGS I MUST DO TODAY
Do the least desired task first!

◇ _____
◇ _____
◇ _____

✦✦✦✦ OTHER TO-DO'S ✦✦✦✦

◇ _____
◇ _____
◇ _____
◇ _____

✦✦✦✦ TASKS TO DELEGATE ✦✦✦✦

◇ _____
◇ _____
◇ _____

✦✦✦✦ HABITS ✦✦✦✦

◇ Visualized My Goal
◇ Exercised
◇ 8 Glasses of Water

♡ ♡ ♡ ♡ ♡ ♡ ♡ ♡

◇ _____
◇ _____
◇ _____

SCHEDULE

4:00	
4:30	
5:00	
5:30	
6:00	
6:30	
7:00	
7:30	
8:00	
8:30	
9:00	
9:30	
10:00	
10:30	
11:00	
11:30	
12:00	
12:30	
1:00	
1:30	
2:00	
2:30	
3:00	
3:30	
4:00	
4:30	
5:00	
5:30	
6:00	
6:30	
7:00	
7:30	
8:00	
8:30	
9:00	
9:30	

End of Day Reflection:

What were your wins today?

What didn't happen & why? How can you fix this moving forward?

Great work today!

Schedule your action plan for tomorrow. →

My Brilliant Ideas or Notes

DAILY ACTION PLAN

DAY 24 OF 90

Date: _____

Morning Review

In 67-days I will: _____
My #1 focus today: _____
I'm grateful for: _____

SUCCESS LIST
3 THINGS I MUST DO TODAY
Do the least desired task first!

◇ _____
◇ _____
◇ _____

✦✦✦✦ **OTHER TO-DO'S** ✦✦✦✦

◇ _____
◇ _____
◇ _____
◇ _____

✦✦✦✦ **TASKS TO DELEGATE** ✦✦✦✦

◇ _____
◇ _____
◇ _____

✦✦✦✦ **HABITS** ✦✦✦✦

◇ Visualized My Goal
◇ Exercised
◇ 8 Glasses of Water
♡ ♡ ♡ ♡ ♡ ♡ ♡ ♡

◇ _____
◇ _____
◇ _____

SCHEDULE

4:00	
4:30	
5:00	
5:30	
6:00	
6:30	
7:00	
7:30	
8:00	
8:30	
9:00	
9:30	
10:00	
10:30	
11:00	
11:30	
12:00	
12:30	
1:00	
1:30	
2:00	
2:30	
3:00	
3:30	
4:00	
4:30	
5:00	
5:30	
6:00	
6:30	
7:00	
7:30	
8:00	
8:30	
9:00	
9:30	

End of Day Reflection:

What were your wins today?

What didn't happen & why? How can you fix this moving forward?

Great work today!

Schedule your action plan for tomorrow. →

My Brilliant Ideas or Notes

DAILY ACTION PLAN

DAY 25 OF 90

Date: _____

Morning Review

In 66-days I will: _____
My #1 focus today: _____
I'm grateful for: _____

SUCCESS LIST
3 THINGS I MUST DO TODAY
Do the least desired task first!

◊ _____

◊ _____

◊ _____

♦♦♦♦ OTHER TO-DO'S ♦♦♦♦
◊ _____
◊ _____
◊ _____
◊ _____

♦♦♦♦ TASKS TO DELEGATE ♦♦♦♦
◊ _____
◊ _____
◊ _____

♦♦♦♦ HABITS ♦♦♦♦
◊ Visualized My Goal
◊ Exercised
◊ 8 Glasses of Water
♡♡♡♡♡♡♡♡
◊ _____
◊ _____
◊ _____

SCHEDULE

4:00	
4:30	
5:00	
5:30	
6:00	
6:30	
7:00	
7:30	
8:00	
8:30	
9:00	
9:30	
10:00	
10:30	
11:00	
11:30	
12:00	
12:30	
1:00	
1:30	
2:00	
2:30	
3:00	
3:30	
4:00	
4:30	
5:00	
5:30	
6:00	
6:30	
7:00	
7:30	
8:00	
8:30	
9:00	
9:30	

End of Day Reflection:

What were your wins today?

What didn't happen & why? How can you fix this moving forward?

Great work today!

Schedule your action plan for tomorrow. →

My Brilliant Ideas or Notes

DAILY ACTION PLAN

DAY 26 OF 90

Date: _____

Morning Review

In 65-days I will: _____
My #1 focus today: _____
I'm grateful for: _____

SUCCESS LIST
3 THINGS I MUST DO TODAY
Do the least desired task first!

◊ _____

◊ _____

◊ _____

◆◆◆◆ OTHER TO-DO'S ◆◆◆◆
◊ _____
◊ _____
◊ _____
◊ _____

◆◆◆◆ TASKS TO DELEGATE ◆◆◆◆
◊ _____
◊ _____
◊ _____

◆◆◆◆ HABITS ◆◆◆◆
◊ Visualized My Goal
◊ Exercised
◊ 8 Glasses of Water
♡ ♡ ♡ ♡ ♡ ♡ ♡ ♡
◊ _____
◊ _____
◊ _____

SCHEDULE

4:00	
4:30	
5:00	
5:30	
6:00	
6:30	
7:00	
7:30	
8:00	
8:30	
9:00	
9:30	
10:00	
10:30	
11:00	
11:30	
12:00	
12:30	
1:00	
1:30	
2:00	
2:30	
3:00	
3:30	
4:00	
4:30	
5:00	
5:30	
6:00	
6:30	
7:00	
7:30	
8:00	
8:30	
9:00	
9:30	

End of Day Reflection:

What were your wins today?

What didn't happen & why? How can you fix this moving forward?

Great work today!

Schedule your action plan for tomorrow. →

My Brilliant Ideas or Notes

DAILY ACTION PLAN

DAY 27 OF 90

Date: _____

Morning Review

In 64-days I will: _____
My #1 focus today: _____
I'm grateful for: _____

SUCCESS LIST
3 THINGS I MUST DO TODAY
Do the least desired task first!

◊ _____

◊ _____

◊ _____

◆◆◆◆◆ OTHER TO-DO'S ◆◆◆◆◆
◊ _____
◊ _____
◊ _____
◊ _____

◆◆◆◆◆ TASKS TO DELEGATE ◆◆◆◆◆
◊ _____
◊ _____
◊ _____

◆◆◆◆◆ HABITS ◆◆◆◆◆
◊ Visualized My Goal
◊ Exercised
◊ 8 Glasses of Water
♡ ♡ ♡ ♡ ♡ ♡ ♡ ♡
◊ _____
◊ _____
◊ _____

SCHEDULE

4:00	
4:30	
5:00	
5:30	
6:00	
6:30	
7:00	
7:30	
8:00	
8:30	
9:00	
9:30	
10:00	
10:30	
11:00	
11:30	
12:00	
12:30	
1:00	
1:30	
2:00	
2:30	
3:00	
3:30	
4:00	
4:30	
5:00	
5:30	
6:00	
6:30	
7:00	
7:30	
8:00	
8:30	
9:00	
9:30	

End of Day Reflection:

What were your wins today?

What didn't happen & why? How can you fix this moving forward?

Great work today!

Schedule your action plan for tomorrow. →

My Brilliant Ideas or Notes

DAILY ACTION PLAN

DAY 28 OF 90

Date: _____

Morning Review

In 63-days I will: _____
My #1 focus today: _____
I'm grateful for: _____

SUCCESS LIST
3 THINGS I MUST DO TODAY
Do the least desired task first!

◊ _____

◊ _____

◊ _____

♦♦♦♦♦ OTHER TO-DO'S ♦♦♦♦♦
◊ _____
◊ _____
◊ _____
◊ _____

♦♦♦♦♦ TASKS TO DELEGATE ♦♦♦♦♦
◊ _____
◊ _____
◊ _____

♦♦♦♦♦ HABITS ♦♦♦♦♦
◊ Visualized My Goal
◊ Exercised
◊ 8 Glasses of Water
♡ ♡ ♡ ♡ ♡ ♡ ♡ ♡
◊ _____
◊ _____
◊ _____

SCHEDULE

4:00	
4:30	
5:00	
5:30	
6:00	
6:30	
7:00	
7:30	
8:00	
8:30	
9:00	
9:30	
10:00	
10:30	
11:00	
11:30	
12:00	
12:30	
1:00	
1:30	
2:00	
2:30	
3:00	
3:30	
4:00	
4:30	
5:00	
5:30	
6:00	
6:30	
7:00	
7:30	
8:00	
8:30	
9:00	
9:30	

End of Day Reflection:

What were your wins today?

What didn't happen & why? How can you fix this moving forward?

Great work today!

Schedule your action plan for tomorrow. →

My Brilliant Ideas or Notes

DAILY ACTION PLAN

DAY 29 OF 90

Date: _____

Morning Review

In 62-days I will: _____
My #1 focus today: _____
I'm grateful for: _____

SUCCESS LIST
3 THINGS I MUST DO TODAY
Do the least desired task first!

◊ _____
◊ _____
◊ _____

♦♦♦♦ OTHER TO-DO'S ♦♦♦♦
◊ _____
◊ _____
◊ _____
◊ _____

♦♦♦♦ TASKS TO DELEGATE ♦♦♦♦
◊ _____
◊ _____
◊ _____

♦♦♦♦ HABITS ♦♦♦♦
◊ Visualized My Goal
◊ Exercised
◊ 8 Glasses of Water
♡ ♡ ♡ ♡ ♡ ♡ ♡ ♡
◊ _____
◊ _____
◊ _____

SCHEDULE

4:00	
4:30	
5:00	
5:30	
6:00	
6:30	
7:00	
7:30	
8:00	
8:30	
9:00	
9:30	
10:00	
10:30	
11:00	
11:30	
12:00	
12:30	
1:00	
1:30	
2:00	
2:30	
3:00	
3:30	
4:00	
4:30	
5:00	
5:30	
6:00	
6:30	
7:00	
7:30	
8:00	
8:30	
9:00	
9:30	

End of Day Reflection:

What were your wins today?

What didn't happen & why? How can you fix this moving forward?

Great work today!

Schedule your action plan for tomorrow. →

My Brilliant Ideas or Notes

DAILY ACTION PLAN

DAY 30 OF 90

Date: _____

Morning Review

In 61-days I will: _____
My #1 focus today: _____
I'm grateful for: _____

SUCCESS LIST
3 THINGS I MUST DO TODAY
Do the least desired task first!

◊ _____

◊ _____

◊ _____

◆◆◆◆◆ OTHER TO-DO'S ◆◆◆◆◆
◊ _____
◊ _____
◊ _____
◊ _____

◆◆◆◆◆ TASKS TO DELEGATE ◆◆◆◆◆
◊ _____
◊ _____
◊ _____

◆◆◆◆◆ HABITS ◆◆◆◆◆
◊ Visualized My Goal
◊ Exercised
◊ 8 Glasses of Water
♡ ♡ ♡ ♡ ♡ ♡ ♡
◊ _____
◊ _____
◊ _____

SCHEDULE

4:00	
4:30	
5:00	
5:30	
6:00	
6:30	
7:00	
7:30	
8:00	
8:30	
9:00	
9:30	
10:00	
10:30	
11:00	
11:30	
12:00	
12:30	
1:00	
1:30	
2:00	
2:30	
3:00	
3:30	
4:00	
4:30	
5:00	
5:30	
6:00	
6:30	
7:00	
7:30	
8:00	
8:30	
9:00	
9:30	

End of Day Reflection:

What were your wins today?

What didn't happen & why? How can you fix this moving forward?

Great work today!

Schedule your action plan for tomorrow. →

My Brilliant Ideas or Notes

ROUND THREE: REFLECTION

DID YOU ACHIEVE YOUR MINI GOAL THIS ROUND?

Don't forget to reward yourself!

———————————

WHAT SURPRISE ACCOMPLISHMENT DID YOU ACHIEVE?

_____
_____

WHAT DIDN'T HAPPEN OR GO AS PLANNED?

_____
_____
_____

HOW CAN YOU FIX THIS SO IT DOESN'T HAPPEN IN THE FUTURE?

_____
_____
_____

WHAT WAS THE MOST VALUABLE LESSON YOU LEARNED?

_____
_____

ARE YOU ON TRACK TO ACCOMPLISHING YOUR GOAL?
IF NOT, WHAT CAN YOU DO TO FIX THIS?

Delegate items or find a way to free up more time.

_____
_____
_____
_____
_____

IS ANYTHING LEFT UNFINISHED?
IF SO, HOW DO YOU PLAN TO COMPLETE IT?

_____
_____
_____
_____
_____

WHAT ARE YOU MOST GRATEFUL FOR?

_____
_____
_____
_____
_____

Great job this round girl! Now let's plan Round Four. →

MINI GOAL PLANNER

ROUND FOUR: DAYS 31-40

IF I SUCCESSFULLY COMPLETE THIS ROUND, I'LL REWARD MYSELF BY:
_____

◆ If a task has more than one action step, break the task down into smaller steps. This will help increase your focus and make it easier to take action.

MINI GOAL: _____

DATE: From _____ **to** _____

Done?	Tasks/Projects to Complete in Order of Sequence	Delegate Task To:
◊		
◊		
◊		
◊		
◊		
◊		
◊		
◊		
◊		
◊		
◊		
◊		
◊		
◊		

DAILY ACTION PLAN

DAY 31 OF 90

Date: _____

Morning Review

In 60-days I will: _____
My #1 focus today: _____
I'm grateful for: _____

SUCCESS LIST
3 THINGS I MUST DO TODAY
Do the least desired task first!

◇ _____
◇ _____
◇ _____

✦✦✦✦ OTHER TO-DO'S ✦✦✦✦

◇ _____
◇ _____
◇ _____
◇ _____

✦✦✦✦ TASKS TO DELEGATE ✦✦✦✦

◇ _____
◇ _____
◇ _____

✦✦✦✦ HABITS ✦✦✦✦

◇ Visualized My Goal
◇ Exercised
◇ 8 Glasses of Water
♡ ♡ ♡ ♡ ♡ ♡ ♡ ♡
◇ _____
◇ _____
◇ _____

SCHEDULE

4:00
4:30
5:00
5:30
6:00
6:30
7:00
7:30
8:00
8:30
9:00
9:30
10:00
10:30
11:00
11:30
12:00
12:30
1:00
1:30
2:00
2:30
3:00
3:30
4:00
4:30
5:00
5:30
6:00
6:30
7:00
7:30
8:00
8:30
9:00
9:30

End of Day Reflection:

What were your wins today?

What didn't happen & why? How can you fix this moving forward?

Great work today!

Schedule your action plan for tomorrow. →

My Brilliant Ideas or Notes

DAILY ACTION PLAN

DAY 32 OF 90

Date: _____

Morning Review

In 59-days I will: _____
My #1 focus today: _____
I'm grateful for: _____

SUCCESS LIST
3 THINGS I MUST DO TODAY
Do the least desired task first!

◊ _____

◊ _____

◊ _____

♦♦♦♦ OTHER TO-DO'S ♦♦♦♦
◊ _____
◊ _____
◊ _____
◊ _____

♦♦♦♦ TASKS TO DELEGATE ♦♦♦♦
◊ _____
◊ _____
◊ _____

♦♦♦♦ HABITS ♦♦♦♦
◊ Visualized My Goal
◊ Exercised
◊ 8 Glasses of Water

♡ ♡ ♡ ♡ ♡ ♡ ♡ ♡

◊ _____
◊ _____
◊ _____

SCHEDULE

4:00	
4:30	
5:00	
5:30	
6:00	
6:30	
7:00	
7:30	
8:00	
8:30	
9:00	
9:30	
10:00	
10:30	
11:00	
11:30	
12:00	
12:30	
1:00	
1:30	
2:00	
2:30	
3:00	
3:30	
4:00	
4:30	
5:00	
5:30	
6:00	
6:30	
7:00	
7:30	
8:00	
8:30	
9:00	
9:30	

End of Day Reflection:

What were your wins today?

What didn't happen & why? How can you fix this moving forward?

Great work today!

Schedule your action plan for tomorrow. →

My Brilliant Ideas or Notes

DAILY ACTION PLAN

DAY 33 OF 90

Date: _____

Morning Review

In 58-days I will: _____
My #1 focus today: _____
I'm grateful for: _____

SUCCESS LIST
3 THINGS I MUST DO TODAY
Do the least desired task first!

◊ _____
◊ _____
◊ _____

♦♦♦♦ OTHER TO-DO'S ♦♦♦♦
◊ _____
◊ _____
◊ _____
◊ _____

♦♦♦♦ TASKS TO DELEGATE ♦♦♦♦
◊ _____
◊ _____
◊ _____

♦♦♦♦ HABITS ♦♦♦♦
◊ Visualized My Goal
◊ Exercised
◊ 8 Glasses of Water
♡ ♡ ♡ ♡ ♡ ♡ ♡ ♡
◊ _____
◊ _____
◊ _____

SCHEDULE

4:00	
4:30	
5:00	
5:30	
6:00	
6:30	
7:00	
7:30	
8:00	
8:30	
9:00	
9:30	
10:00	
10:30	
11:00	
11:30	
12:00	
12:30	
1:00	
1:30	
2:00	
2:30	
3:00	
3:30	
4:00	
4:30	
5:00	
5:30	
6:00	
6:30	
7:00	
7:30	
8:00	
8:30	
9:00	
9:30	

End of Day Reflection:

What were your wins today?

What didn't happen & why? How can you fix this moving forward?

Great work today!

Schedule your action plan for tomorrow. →

My Brilliant Ideas or Notes

DAILY ACTION PLAN

DAY 34 OF 90

Date: _____

Morning Review

In 57-days I will: _____
My #1 focus today: _____
I'm grateful for: _____

SUCCESS LIST
3 THINGS I MUST DO TODAY
Do the least desired task first!

◇ _____

◇ _____

◇ _____

♦♦♦♦ OTHER TO-DO'S ♦♦♦♦
◇ _____
◇ _____
◇ _____
◇ _____

♦♦♦♦ TASKS TO DELEGATE ♦♦♦♦
◇ _____
◇ _____
◇ _____

♦♦♦♦ HABITS ♦♦♦♦
◇ Visualized My Goal
◇ Exercised
◇ 8 Glasses of Water
♡ ♡ ♡ ♡ ♡ ♡ ♡ ♡
◇ _____
◇ _____
◇ _____

SCHEDULE

4:00	
4:30	
5:00	
5:30	
6:00	
6:30	
7:00	
7:30	
8:00	
8:30	
9:00	
9:30	
10:00	
10:30	
11:00	
11:30	
12:00	
12:30	
1:00	
1:30	
2:00	
2:30	
3:00	
3:30	
4:00	
4:30	
5:00	
5:30	
6:00	
6:30	
7:00	
7:30	
8:00	
8:30	
9:00	
9:30	

End of Day Reflection:

What were your wins today?

What didn't happen & why? How can you fix this moving forward?

Great work today!

Schedule your action plan for tomorrow. →

My Brilliant Ideas or Notes

DAILY ACTION PLAN

DAY 35 OF 90

Date: _____

Morning Review

In 56-days I will: _____
My #1 focus today: _____
I'm grateful for: _____

SUCCESS LIST
3 THINGS I MUST DO TODAY
Do the least desired task first!

◊ _____

◊ _____

◊ _____

♦♦♦♦ OTHER TO-DO'S ♦♦♦♦
◊ _____
◊ _____
◊ _____
◊ _____

♦♦♦♦ TASKS TO DELEGATE ♦♦♦♦
◊ _____
◊ _____
◊ _____

♦♦♦♦ HABITS ♦♦♦♦
◊ Visualized My Goal
◊ Exercised
◊ 8 Glasses of Water
♡ ♡ ♡ ♡ ♡ ♡ ♡ ♡
◊ _____
◊ _____
◊ _____

SCHEDULE

4:00	
4:30	
5:00	
5:30	
6:00	
6:30	
7:00	
7:30	
8:00	
8:30	
9:00	
9:30	
10:00	
10:30	
11:00	
11:30	
12:00	
12:30	
1:00	
1:30	
2:00	
2:30	
3:00	
3:30	
4:00	
4:30	
5:00	
5:30	
6:00	
6:30	
7:00	
7:30	
8:00	
8:30	
9:00	
9:30	

End of Day Reflection:

What were your wins today?

What didn't happen & why? How can you fix this moving forward?

Great work today!

Schedule your action plan for tomorrow. →

My Brilliant Ideas or Notes

DAILY ACTION PLAN

DAY 36 OF 90

Date: _____

Morning Review

In 55-days I will: _____
My #1 focus today: _____
I'm grateful for: _____

SUCCESS LIST
3 THINGS I MUST DO TODAY
Do the least desired task first!

◊ _____
◊ _____
◊ _____

♦♦♦♦ OTHER TO-DO'S ♦♦♦♦
◊ _____
◊ _____
◊ _____
◊ _____

♦♦♦♦ TASKS TO DELEGATE ♦♦♦♦
◊ _____
◊ _____
◊ _____

♦♦♦♦ HABITS ♦♦♦♦
◊ Visualized My Goal
◊ Exercised
◊ 8 Glasses of Water
♡ ♡ ♡ ♡ ♡ ♡ ♡ ♡

◊ _____
◊ _____
◊ _____

SCHEDULE

4:00
4:30
5:00
5:30
6:00
6:30
7:00
7:30
8:00
8:30
9:00
9:30
10:00
10:30
11:00
11:30
12:00
12:30
1:00
1:30
2:00
2:30
3:00
3:30
4:00
4:30
5:00
5:30
6:00
6:30
7:00
7:30
8:00
8:30
9:00
9:30

End of Day Reflection:

What were your wins today?

What didn't happen & why? How can you fix this moving forward?

Great work today!

Schedule your action plan for tomorrow. →

My Brilliant Ideas or Notes

DAILY ACTION PLAN

DAY 37 OF 90

Date: _____

Morning Review

In 54-days I will: _____
My #1 focus today: _____
I'm grateful for: _____

SUCCESS LIST
3 THINGS I MUST DO TODAY
Do the least desired task first!

◊ _____

◊ _____

◊ _____

♦♦♦♦♦ OTHER TO-DO'S ♦♦♦♦♦
◊ _____
◊ _____
◊ _____
◊ _____

♦♦♦♦♦ TASKS TO DELEGATE ♦♦♦♦♦
◊ _____
◊ _____
◊ _____

♦♦♦♦♦ HABITS ♦♦♦♦♦
◊ Visualized My Goal
◊ Exercised
◊ 8 Glasses of Water
♡ ♡ ♡ ♡ ♡ ♡ ♡ ♡
◊ _____
◊ _____
◊ _____

SCHEDULE

4:00	
4:30	
5:00	
5:30	
6:00	
6:30	
7:00	
7:30	
8:00	
8:30	
9:00	
9:30	
10:00	
10:30	
11:00	
11:30	
12:00	
12:30	
1:00	
1:30	
2:00	
2:30	
3:00	
3:30	
4:00	
4:30	
5:00	
5:30	
6:00	
6:30	
7:00	
7:30	
8:00	
8:30	
9:00	
9:30	

End of Day Reflection:

What were your wins today?

What didn't happen & why? How can you fix this moving forward?

Great work today!

Schedule your action plan for tomorrow. →

My Brilliant Ideas or Notes

DAILY ACTION PLAN

DAY 38 OF 90

Date: _____

Morning Review

In 53-days I will: _____
My #1 focus today: _____
I'm grateful for: _____

SUCCESS LIST
3 THINGS I MUST DO TODAY
Do the least desired task first!

◊ _____

◊ _____

◊ _____

♦♦♦♦ OTHER TO-DO'S ♦♦♦♦
◊ _____
◊ _____
◊ _____
◊ _____

♦♦♦♦ TASKS TO DELEGATE ♦♦♦♦
◊ _____
◊ _____
◊ _____

♦♦♦♦ HABITS ♦♦♦♦
◊ Visualized My Goal
◊ Exercised
◊ 8 Glasses of Water
♡ ♡ ♡ ♡ ♡ ♡ ♡ ♡
◊ _____
◊ _____
◊ _____

SCHEDULE
- 4:00
- 4:30
- 5:00
- 5:30
- 6:00
- 6:30
- 7:00
- 7:30
- 8:00
- 8:30
- 9:00
- 9:30
- 10:00
- 10:30
- 11:00
- 11:30
- 12:00
- 12:30
- 1:00
- 1:30
- 2:00
- 2:30
- 3:00
- 3:30
- 4:00
- 4:30
- 5:00
- 5:30
- 6:00
- 6:30
- 7:00
- 7:30
- 8:00
- 8:30
- 9:00
- 9:30

End of Day Reflection:

What were your wins today?

What didn't happen & why? How can you fix this moving forward?

Great work today!

Schedule your action plan for tomorrow. →

My Brilliant Ideas or Notes

DAILY ACTION PLAN

DAY 39 OF 90

Date: _____

Morning Review

In 52-days I will: _____
My #1 focus today: _____
I'm grateful for: _____

SUCCESS LIST
3 THINGS I MUST DO TODAY
Do the least desired task first!

◊ _____

◊ _____

◊ _____

♦♦♦♦♦ OTHER TO-DO'S ♦♦♦♦♦

◊ _____
◊ _____
◊ _____
◊ _____

♦♦♦♦♦ TASKS TO DELEGATE ♦♦♦♦♦

◊ _____
◊ _____
◊ _____

♦♦♦♦♦ HABITS ♦♦♦♦♦

◊ Visualized My Goal
◊ Exercised
◊ 8 Glasses of Water
♡ ♡ ♡ ♡ ♡ ♡ ♡ ♡

◊ _____
◊ _____
◊ _____

SCHEDULE

4:00
4:30
5:00
5:30
6:00
6:30
7:00
7:30
8:00
8:30
9:00
9:30
10:00
10:30
11:00
11:30
12:00
12:30
1:00
1:30
2:00
2:30
3:00
3:30
4:00
4:30
5:00
5:30
6:00
6:30
7:00
7:30
8:00
8:30
9:00
9:30

End of Day Reflection:

What were your wins today?

What didn't happen & why? How can you fix this moving forward?

Great work today!

Schedule your action plan for tomorrow. →

My Brilliant Ideas or Notes

DAILY ACTION PLAN

DAY 40 OF 90

Date: _____

Morning Review

In 51-days I will: _____
My #1 focus today: _____
I'm grateful for: _____

SUCCESS LIST
3 THINGS I MUST DO TODAY
Do the least desired task first!

◊ _____

◊ _____

◊ _____

♦♦♦♦ OTHER TO-DO'S ♦♦♦♦
◊ _____
◊ _____
◊ _____
◊ _____

♦♦♦♦ TASKS TO DELEGATE ♦♦♦♦
◊ _____
◊ _____
◊ _____

♦♦♦♦ HABITS ♦♦♦♦
◊ Visualized My Goal
◊ Exercised
◊ 8 Glasses of Water
♡♡♡♡♡♡♡♡
◊ _____
◊ _____
◊ _____

SCHEDULE

4:00	
4:30	
5:00	
5:30	
6:00	
6:30	
7:00	
7:30	
8:00	
8:30	
9:00	
9:30	
10:00	
10:30	
11:00	
11:30	
12:00	
12:30	
1:00	
1:30	
2:00	
2:30	
3:00	
3:30	
4:00	
4:30	
5:00	
5:30	
6:00	
6:30	
7:00	
7:30	
8:00	
8:30	
9:00	
9:30	

End of Day Reflection:

What were your wins today?

What didn't happen & why? How can you fix this moving forward?

Great work today!

Schedule your action plan for tomorrow. →

My Brilliant Ideas or Notes

ROUND FOUR: REFLECTION

DID YOU ACHIEVE YOUR MINI GOAL THIS ROUND?

Don't forget to reward yourself!

_____

WHAT SURPRISE ACCOMPLISHMENT DID YOU ACHIEVE?

_____
_____

WHAT DIDN'T HAPPEN OR GO AS PLANNED?

_____
_____
_____

HOW CAN YOU FIX THIS SO IT DOESN'T HAPPEN IN THE FUTURE?

_____
_____
_____
_____

WHAT WAS THE MOST VALUABLE LESSON YOU LEARNED?

_____
_____

GLAMIFY YOUR GOAL

ARE YOU ON TRACK TO ACCOMPLISHING YOUR GOAL?
IF NOT, WHAT CAN YOU DO TO FIX THIS?

Delegate items or find a way to free up more time.

___
___
___
___
___

IS ANYTHING LEFT UNFINISHED?
IF SO, HOW DO YOU PLAN TO COMPLETE IT?

___
___
___
___

WHAT ARE YOU MOST GRATEFUL FOR?

___
___
___
___

Great job this round girl! Now let's plan Round Five. →

MINI GOAL PLANNER

ROUND FIVE: DAYS 41–50

IF I SUCCESSFULLY COMPLETE THIS ROUND, I'LL REWARD MYSELF BY:

_____

♦ If a task has more than one action step, break the task down into smaller steps. This will help increase your focus and make it easier to take action.

MINI GOAL: _____

DATE: From _____ **to** _____

Done?	Tasks/Projects to Complete in Order of Sequence	Delegate Task To:
◊		
◊		
◊		
◊		
◊		
◊		
◊		
◊		
◊		
◊		
◊		
◊		
◊		
◊		

DAILY ACTION PLAN

DAY 41 OF 90

Date: _____

Morning Review

In 50-days I will: _____
My #1 focus today: _____
I'm grateful for: _____

SUCCESS LIST
3 THINGS I MUST DO TODAY
Do the least desired task first!

◊ _____

◊ _____

◊ _____

♦♦♦♦ OTHER TO-DO'S ♦♦♦♦
◊ _____
◊ _____
◊ _____
◊ _____

♦♦♦♦ TASKS TO DELEGATE ♦♦♦♦
◊ _____
◊ _____
◊ _____

♦♦♦♦ HABITS ♦♦♦♦
◊ Visualized My Goal
◊ Exercised
◊ 8 Glasses of Water
♡ ♡ ♡ ♡ ♡ ♡ ♡ ♡

◊ _____
◊ _____
◊ _____

SCHEDULE

4:00	
4:30	
5:00	
5:30	
6:00	
6:30	
7:00	
7:30	
8:00	
8:30	
9:00	
9:30	
10:00	
10:30	
11:00	
11:30	
12:00	
12:30	
1:00	
1:30	
2:00	
2:30	
3:00	
3:30	
4:00	
4:30	
5:00	
5:30	
6:00	
6:30	
7:00	
7:30	
8:00	
8:30	
9:00	
9:30	

End of Day Reflection:

What were your wins today?

What didn't happen & why? How can you fix this moving forward?

Great work today!

Schedule your action plan for tomorrow. →

My Brilliant Ideas or Notes

DAILY ACTION PLAN

DAY 42 OF 90

Date: _____

Morning Review

In 49-days I will: _____
My #1 focus today: _____
I'm grateful for: _____

SUCCESS LIST
3 THINGS I MUST DO TODAY
Do the least desired task first!

◊ _____

◊ _____

◊ _____

✦✦✦✦ OTHER TO-DO'S ✦✦✦✦

◊ _____
◊ _____
◊ _____
◊ _____

✦✦✦✦ TASKS TO DELEGATE ✦✦✦✦

◊ _____
◊ _____
◊ _____

✦✦✦✦ HABITS ✦✦✦✦

◊ Visualized My Goal
◊ Exercised
◊ 8 Glasses of Water
♡ ♡ ♡ ♡ ♡ ♡ ♡ ♡

◊ _____
◊ _____
◊ _____

SCHEDULE

4:00
4:30
5:00
5:30
6:00
6:30
7:00
7:30
8:00
8:30
9:00
9:30
10:00
10:30
11:00
11:30
12:00
12:30
1:00
1:30
2:00
2:30
3:00
3:30
4:00
4:30
5:00
5:30
6:00
6:30
7:00
7:30
8:00
8:30
9:00
9:30

End of Day Reflection:

What were your wins today?

What didn't happen & why? How can you fix this moving forward?

Great work today!

Schedule your action plan for tomorrow. →

My Brilliant Ideas or Notes

DAILY ACTION PLAN

DAY 43 OF 90

Date: _____

Morning Review

In 48-days I will: _____
My #1 focus today: _____
I'm grateful for: _____

SUCCESS LIST
3 THINGS I MUST DO TODAY
Do the least desired task first!

◇ _____

◇ _____

◇ _____

♦♦♦♦ OTHER TO-DO'S ♦♦♦♦

◇ _____
◇ _____
◇ _____
◇ _____

♦♦♦♦ TASKS TO DELEGATE ♦♦♦♦

◇ _____
◇ _____
◇ _____

♦♦♦♦ HABITS ♦♦♦♦

◇ Visualized My Goal
◇ Exercised
◇ 8 Glasses of Water
♡ ♡ ♡ ♡ ♡ ♡ ♡ ♡

◇ _____
◇ _____
◇ _____

SCHEDULE

4:00	
4:30	
5:00	
5:30	
6:00	
6:30	
7:00	
7:30	
8:00	
8:30	
9:00	
9:30	
10:00	
10:30	
11:00	
11:30	
12:00	
12:30	
1:00	
1:30	
2:00	
2:30	
3:00	
3:30	
4:00	
4:30	
5:00	
5:30	
6:00	
6:30	
7:00	
7:30	
8:00	
8:30	
9:00	
9:30	

End of Day Reflection:

What were your wins today?

What didn't happen & why? How can you fix this moving forward?

Great work today!

Schedule your action plan for tomorrow. →

My Brilliant Ideas or Notes

DAILY ACTION PLAN

DAY 44 OF 90

Date: _____

Morning Review

In 47-days I will: _____
My #1 focus today: _____
I'm grateful for: _____

SUCCESS LIST
3 THINGS I MUST DO TODAY
Do the least desired task first!

◊ _____
◊ _____
◊ _____

✦✦✦✦ OTHER TO-DO'S ✦✦✦✦
◊ _____
◊ _____
◊ _____
◊ _____

✦✦✦✦ TASKS TO DELEGATE ✦✦✦✦
◊ _____
◊ _____
◊ _____

✦✦✦✦ HABITS ✦✦✦✦
◊ Visualized My Goal
◊ Exercised
◊ 8 Glasses of Water
♡ ♡ ♡ ♡ ♡ ♡ ♡ ♡
◊ _____
◊ _____
◊ _____

SCHEDULE

4:00	
4:30	
5:00	
5:30	
6:00	
6:30	
7:00	
7:30	
8:00	
8:30	
9:00	
9:30	
10:00	
10:30	
11:00	
11:30	
12:00	
12:30	
1:00	
1:30	
2:00	
2:30	
3:00	
3:30	
4:00	
4:30	
5:00	
5:30	
6:00	
6:30	
7:00	
7:30	
8:00	
8:30	
9:00	
9:30	

End of Day Reflection:

What were your wins today?

What didn't happen & why? How can you fix this moving forward?

Great work today!

Schedule your action plan for tomorrow. →

My Brilliant Ideas or Notes

DAILY ACTION PLAN

DAY 45 OF 90

Date: _____

Morning Review

In 46-days I will: _____
My #1 focus today: _____
I'm grateful for: _____

SUCCESS LIST
3 THINGS I MUST DO TODAY
Do the least desired task first!

◊ _____
◊ _____
◊ _____

♦♦♦♦♦ OTHER TO-DO'S ♦♦♦♦♦
◊ _____
◊ _____
◊ _____
◊ _____

♦♦♦♦♦ TASKS TO DELEGATE ♦♦♦♦♦
◊ _____
◊ _____
◊ _____

♦♦♦♦♦ HABITS ♦♦♦♦♦
◊ Visualized My Goal
◊ Exercised
◊ 8 Glasses of Water
♡ ♡ ♡ ♡ ♡ ♡ ♡ ♡
◊ _____
◊ _____
◊ _____

SCHEDULE

4:00	
4:30	
5:00	
5:30	
6:00	
6:30	
7:00	
7:30	
8:00	
8:30	
9:00	
9:30	
10:00	
10:30	
11:00	
11:30	
12:00	
12:30	
1:00	
1:30	
2:00	
2:30	
3:00	
3:30	
4:00	
4:30	
5:00	
5:30	
6:00	
6:30	
7:00	
7:30	
8:00	
8:30	
9:00	
9:30	

End of Day Reflection:

What were your wins today?

What didn't happen & why? How can you fix this moving forward?

Great work today!

Schedule your action plan for tomorrow. →

My Brilliant Ideas or Notes

DAILY ACTION PLAN

DAY 46 OF 90

Date: _____

Morning Review

In 45-days I will: _____
My #1 focus today: _____
I'm grateful for: _____

SUCCESS LIST
3 THINGS I MUST DO TODAY
Do the least desired task first!

◊ _____
◊ _____
◊ _____

♦♦♦♦ OTHER TO-DO'S ♦♦♦♦

◊ _____
◊ _____
◊ _____
◊ _____

♦♦♦♦ TASKS TO DELEGATE ♦♦♦♦

◊ _____
◊ _____
◊ _____

♦♦♦♦ HABITS ♦♦♦♦

◊ Visualized My Goal
◊ Exercised
◊ 8 Glasses of Water
♡ ♡ ♡ ♡ ♡ ♡ ♡ ♡
◊ _____
◊ _____
◊ _____

SCHEDULE

4:00	
4:30	
5:00	
5:30	
6:00	
6:30	
7:00	
7:30	
8:00	
8:30	
9:00	
9:30	
10:00	
10:30	
11:00	
11:30	
12:00	
12:30	
1:00	
1:30	
2:00	
2:30	
3:00	
3:30	
4:00	
4:30	
5:00	
5:30	
6:00	
6:30	
7:00	
7:30	
8:00	
8:30	
9:00	
9:30	

End of Day Reflection:

What were your wins today?

What didn't happen & why? How can you fix this moving forward?

Great work today!

Schedule your action plan for tomorrow. →

My Brilliant Ideas or Notes

DAILY ACTION PLAN

DAY 47 OF 90

Date: _____

Morning Review

In 44-days I will: _____
My #1 focus today: _____
I'm grateful for: _____

SUCCESS LIST
3 THINGS I MUST DO TODAY
Do the least desired task first!

◊ _____

◊ _____

◊ _____

♦♦♦♦ OTHER TO-DO'S ♦♦♦♦
◊ _____
◊ _____
◊ _____
◊ _____

♦♦♦♦ TASKS TO DELEGATE ♦♦♦♦
◊ _____
◊ _____
◊ _____

♦♦♦♦ HABITS ♦♦♦♦
◊ Visualized My Goal
◊ Exercised
◊ 8 Glasses of Water
♡ ♡ ♡ ♡ ♡ ♡ ♡ ♡
◊ _____
◊ _____
◊ _____

SCHEDULE

4:00	
4:30	
5:00	
5:30	
6:00	
6:30	
7:00	
7:30	
8:00	
8:30	
9:00	
9:30	
10:00	
10:30	
11:00	
11:30	
12:00	
12:30	
1:00	
1:30	
2:00	
2:30	
3:00	
3:30	
4:00	
4:30	
5:00	
5:30	
6:00	
6:30	
7:00	
7:30	
8:00	
8:30	
9:00	
9:30	

End of Day Reflection:

What were your wins today?

What didn't happen & why? How can you fix this moving forward?

Great work today!

Schedule your action plan for tomorrow. →

My Brilliant Ideas or Notes

DAILY ACTION PLAN

DAY 48 OF 90

Date: _____

Morning Review

In 43-days I will: _____
My #1 focus today: _____
I'm grateful for: _____

SUCCESS LIST
3 THINGS I MUST DO TODAY
Do the least desired task first!

◊ _____

◊ _____

◊ _____

♦♦♦♦ OTHER TO-DO'S ♦♦♦♦

◊ _____
◊ _____
◊ _____
◊ _____

♦♦♦♦ TASKS TO DELEGATE ♦♦♦♦

◊ _____
◊ _____
◊ _____

♦♦♦♦ HABITS ♦♦♦♦
◊ Visualized My Goal
◊ Exercised
◊ 8 Glasses of Water
♡ ♡ ♡ ♡ ♡ ♡ ♡ ♡
◊ _____
◊ _____
◊ _____

SCHEDULE

4:00	
4:30	
5:00	
5:30	
6:00	
6:30	
7:00	
7:30	
8:00	
8:30	
9:00	
9:30	
10:00	
10:30	
11:00	
11:30	
12:00	
12:30	
1:00	
1:30	
2:00	
2:30	
3:00	
3:30	
4:00	
4:30	
5:00	
5:30	
6:00	
6:30	
7:00	
7:30	
8:00	
8:30	
9:00	
9:30	

End of Day Reflection:

What were your wins today?

What didn't happen & why? How can you fix this moving forward?

Great work today!

Schedule your action plan for tomorrow. →

My Brilliant Ideas or Notes

DAILY ACTION PLAN

DAY 49 OF 90
Date: _____

Morning Review

In 42-days I will: _____
My #1 focus today: _____
I'm grateful for: _____

SUCCESS LIST
3 THINGS I MUST DO TODAY
Do the least desired task first!

◇ _____
◇ _____
◇ _____

✦✦✦✦ OTHER TO-DO'S ✦✦✦✦

◇ _____
◇ _____
◇ _____
◇ _____

✦✦✦✦ TASKS TO DELEGATE ✦✦✦✦

◇ _____
◇ _____
◇ _____

✦✦✦✦ HABITS ✦✦✦✦

◇ Visualized My Goal
◇ Exercised
◇ 8 Glasses of Water
♡ ♡ ♡ ♡ ♡ ♡ ♡ ♡

◇ _____
◇ _____
◇ _____

SCHEDULE

4:00
4:30
5:00
5:30
6:00
6:30
7:00
7:30
8:00
8:30
9:00
9:30
10:00
10:30
11:00
11:30
12:00
12:30
1:00
1:30
2:00
2:30
3:00
3:30
4:00
4:30
5:00
5:30
6:00
6:30
7:00
7:30
8:00
8:30
9:00
9:30

End of Day Reflection:

What were your wins today?

What didn't happen & why? How can you fix this moving forward?

Great work today!

Schedule your action plan for tomorrow. →

My Brilliant Ideas or Notes

DAILY ACTION PLAN

DAY 50 OF 90

Date: _____

Morning Review

In 41-days I will: _____
My #1 focus today: _____
I'm grateful for: _____

SUCCESS LIST
3 THINGS I MUST DO TODAY
Do the least desired task first!

◊ _____

◊ _____

◊ _____

◆◆◆◆◆ OTHER TO-DO'S ◆◆◆◆◆
◊ _____
◊ _____
◊ _____
◊ _____

◆◆◆◆◆ TASKS TO DELEGATE ◆◆◆◆◆
◊ _____
◊ _____
◊ _____

◆◆◆◆◆ HABITS ◆◆◆◆◆
◊ Visualized My Goal
◊ Exercised
◊ 8 Glasses of Water
♡ ♡ ♡ ♡ ♡ ♡ ♡ ♡
◊ _____
◊ _____
◊ _____

SCHEDULE

4:00	
4:30	
5:00	
5:30	
6:00	
6:30	
7:00	
7:30	
8:00	
8:30	
9:00	
9:30	
10:00	
10:30	
11:00	
11:30	
12:00	
12:30	
1:00	
1:30	
2:00	
2:30	
3:00	
3:30	
4:00	
4:30	
5:00	
5:30	
6:00	
6:30	
7:00	
7:30	
8:00	
8:30	
9:00	
9:30	

End of Day Reflection:

What were your wins today?

What didn't happen & why? How can you fix this moving forward?

Great work today!

Schedule your action plan for tomorrow. →

My Brilliant Ideas or Notes

ROUND FIVE: REFLECTION

DID YOU ACHIEVE YOUR MINI GOAL THIS ROUND?

Don't forget to reward yourself!

_____

WHAT SURPRISE ACCOMPLISHMENT DID YOU ACHIEVE?

_____

_____

WHAT DIDN'T HAPPEN OR GO AS PLANNED?

_____

_____

_____

HOW CAN YOU FIX THIS SO IT DOESN'T HAPPEN IN THE FUTURE?

_____

_____

_____

WHAT WAS THE MOST VALUABLE LESSON YOU LEARNED?

_____

_____

ARE YOU ON TRACK TO ACCOMPLISHING YOUR GOAL?
IF NOT, WHAT CAN YOU DO TO FIX THIS?

Delegate items or find a way to free up more time.

___

IS ANYTHING LEFT UNFINISHED?
IF SO, HOW DO YOU PLAN TO COMPLETE IT?

___

WHAT ARE YOU MOST GRATEFUL FOR?

___

Great job this round girl! Now let's plan Round Six. →

MINI GOAL PLANNER

ROUND SIX: DAYS 51-60

IF I SUCCESSFULLY COMPLETE THIS ROUND, I'LL REWARD MYSELF BY:
_____

◆ If a task has more than one action step, break the task down into smaller steps. This will help increase your focus and make it easier to take action.

MINI GOAL: _____

DATE: From _____ **to** _____

Done?	Tasks/Projects to Complete in Order of Sequence	Delegate Task To:
◊		
◊		
◊		
◊		
◊		
◊		
◊		
◊		
◊		
◊		
◊		
◊		
◊		
◊		

DAILY ACTION PLAN

DAY 51 OF 90

Date: _____

Morning Review

In 40-days I will: _____
My #1 focus today: _____
I'm grateful for: _____

SUCCESS LIST
3 THINGS I MUST DO TODAY
Do the least desired task first!

◊ _____

◊ _____

◊ _____

♦♦♦♦♦ OTHER TO-DO'S ♦♦♦♦♦

◊ _____
◊ _____
◊ _____
◊ _____

♦♦♦♦♦ TASKS TO DELEGATE ♦♦♦♦♦

◊ _____
◊ _____
◊ _____

♦♦♦♦♦ HABITS ♦♦♦♦♦

◊ Visualized My Goal
◊ Exercised
◊ 8 Glasses of Water
♡ ♡ ♡ ♡ ♡ ♡ ♡ ♡

◊ _____
◊ _____
◊ _____

SCHEDULE

4:00
4:30
5:00
5:30
6:00
6:30
7:00
7:30
8:00
8:30
9:00
9:30
10:00
10:30
11:00
11:30
12:00
12:30
1:00
1:30
2:00
2:30
3:00
3:30
4:00
4:30
5:00
5:30
6:00
6:30
7:00
7:30
8:00
8:30
9:00
9:30

End of Day Reflection:

What were your wins today?

What didn't happen & why? How can you fix this moving forward?

Great work today!

Schedule your action plan for tomorrow. →

My Brilliant Ideas or Notes

DAILY ACTION PLAN

DAY 52 OF 90

Date: _____

Morning Review

In 39-days I will: _____
My #1 focus today: _____
I'm grateful for: _____

SUCCESS LIST
3 THINGS I MUST DO TODAY
Do the least desired task first!

◇ _____

◇ _____

◇ _____

♦♦♦♦ OTHER TO-DO'S ♦♦♦♦
◇ _____
◇ _____
◇ _____
◇ _____

♦♦♦♦ TASKS TO DELEGATE ♦♦♦♦
◇ _____
◇ _____
◇ _____

♦♦♦♦ HABITS ♦♦♦♦
◇ Visualized My Goal
◇ Exercised
◇ 8 Glasses of Water
♡ ♡ ♡ ♡ ♡ ♡ ♡ ♡
◇ _____
◇ _____
◇ _____

SCHEDULE

4:00	
4:30	
5:00	
5:30	
6:00	
6:30	
7:00	
7:30	
8:00	
8:30	
9:00	
9:30	
10:00	
10:30	
11:00	
11:30	
12:00	
12:30	
1:00	
1:30	
2:00	
2:30	
3:00	
3:30	
4:00	
4:30	
5:00	
5:30	
6:00	
6:30	
7:00	
7:30	
8:00	
8:30	
9:00	
9:30	

End of Day Reflection:

What were your wins today?

What didn't happen & why? How can you fix this moving forward?

Great work today!

Schedule your action plan for tomorrow. →

My Brilliant Ideas or Notes

DAILY ACTION PLAN

DAY 53 OF 90

Date: _____

Morning Review

In 38-days I will: _____
My #1 focus today: _____
I'm grateful for: _____

SUCCESS LIST
3 THINGS I MUST DO TODAY
Do the least desired task first!

◇ _____

◇ _____

◇ _____

♦♦♦♦ OTHER TO-DO'S ♦♦♦♦

◇ _____
◇ _____
◇ _____
◇ _____

♦♦♦♦ TASKS TO DELEGATE ♦♦♦♦

◇ _____
◇ _____
◇ _____

♦♦♦♦ HABITS ♦♦♦♦

◇ Visualized My Goal
◇ Exercised
◇ 8 Glasses of Water
♡♡♡♡♡♡♡♡
◇ _____
◇ _____
◇ _____

SCHEDULE

4:00	
4:30	
5:00	
5:30	
6:00	
6:30	
7:00	
7:30	
8:00	
8:30	
9:00	
9:30	
10:00	
10:30	
11:00	
11:30	
12:00	
12:30	
1:00	
1:30	
2:00	
2:30	
3:00	
3:30	
4:00	
4:30	
5:00	
5:30	
6:00	
6:30	
7:00	
7:30	
8:00	
8:30	
9:00	
9:30	

End of Day Reflection:

What were your wins today?

What didn't happen & why? How can you fix this moving forward?

Great work today!

Schedule your action plan for tomorrow. →

My Brilliant Ideas or Notes

DAILY ACTION PLAN

DAY 54 OF 90
Date: _____

Morning Review

In 37-days I will: _____
My #1 focus today: _____
I'm grateful for: _____

SUCCESS LIST
3 THINGS I MUST DO TODAY
Do the least desired task first!

◊ _____
◊ _____
◊ _____

◆◆◆◆◆ OTHER TO-DO'S ◆◆◆◆◆
◊ _____
◊ _____
◊ _____
◊ _____

◆◆◆◆◆ TASKS TO DELEGATE ◆◆◆◆◆
◊ _____
◊ _____
◊ _____

◆◆◆◆◆ HABITS ◆◆◆◆◆
◊ Visualized My Goal
◊ Exercised
◊ 8 Glasses of Water
♡ ♡ ♡ ♡ ♡ ♡ ♡ ♡
◊ _____
◊ _____
◊ _____

SCHEDULE

4:00	
4:30	
5:00	
5:30	
6:00	
6:30	
7:00	
7:30	
8:00	
8:30	
9:00	
9:30	
10:00	
10:30	
11:00	
11:30	
12:00	
12:30	
1:00	
1:30	
2:00	
2:30	
3:00	
3:30	
4:00	
4:30	
5:00	
5:30	
6:00	
6:30	
7:00	
7:30	
8:00	
8:30	
9:00	
9:30	

End of Day Reflection:

What were your wins today?

What didn't happen & why? How can you fix this moving forward?

Great work today!

Schedule your action plan for tomorrow. →

My Brilliant Ideas or Notes

DAILY ACTION PLAN

DAY 55 OF 90

Date: _____

Morning Review

In 36-days I will: _____
My #1 focus today: _____
I'm grateful for: _____

SUCCESS LIST
3 THINGS I MUST DO TODAY
Do the least desired task first!

◊ _____
◊ _____
◊ _____

◆◆◆◆◆ OTHER TO-DO'S ◆◆◆◆◆

◊ _____
◊ _____
◊ _____
◊ _____

◆◆◆◆◆ TASKS TO DELEGATE ◆◆◆◆◆

◊ _____
◊ _____
◊ _____

◆◆◆◆◆ HABITS ◆◆◆◆◆

◊ Visualized My Goal
◊ Exercised
◊ 8 Glasses of Water
♡ ♡ ♡ ♡ ♡ ♡ ♡ ♡
◊ _____
◊ _____
◊ _____

SCHEDULE

4:00	
4:30	
5:00	
5:30	
6:00	
6:30	
7:00	
7:30	
8:00	
8:30	
9:00	
9:30	
10:00	
10:30	
11:00	
11:30	
12:00	
12:30	
1:00	
1:30	
2:00	
2:30	
3:00	
3:30	
4:00	
4:30	
5:00	
5:30	
6:00	
6:30	
7:00	
7:30	
8:00	
8:30	
9:00	
9:30	

End of Day Reflection:

What were your wins today?

What didn't happen & why? How can you fix this moving forward?

Great work today!

Schedule your action plan for tomorrow. →

My Brilliant Ideas or Notes

DAILY ACTION PLAN

DAY 56 OF 90

Date: _____

Morning Review

In 35-days I will: _____
My #1 focus today: _____
I'm grateful for: _____

SUCCESS LIST
3 THINGS I MUST DO TODAY
Do the least desired task first!

◇ _____

◇ _____

◇ _____

♦♦♦♦♦ OTHER TO-DO'S ♦♦♦♦♦
◇ _____
◇ _____
◇ _____
◇ _____

♦♦♦♦♦ TASKS TO DELEGATE ♦♦♦♦♦
◇ _____
◇ _____
◇ _____

♦♦♦♦♦ HABITS ♦♦♦♦♦
◇ Visualized My Goal
◇ Exercised
◇ 8 Glasses of Water
♡ ♡ ♡ ♡ ♡ ♡ ♡ ♡
◇ _____
◇ _____
◇ _____

SCHEDULE

4:00	
4:30	
5:00	
5:30	
6:00	
6:30	
7:00	
7:30	
8:00	
8:30	
9:00	
9:30	
10:00	
10:30	
11:00	
11:30	
12:00	
12:30	
1:00	
1:30	
2:00	
2:30	
3:00	
3:30	
4:00	
4:30	
5:00	
5:30	
6:00	
6:30	
7:00	
7:30	
8:00	
8:30	
9:00	
9:30	

End of Day Reflection:

What were your wins today?

What didn't happen & why? How can you fix this moving forward?

Great work today!

Schedule your action plan for tomorrow. →

My Brilliant Ideas or Notes

DAILY ACTION PLAN

DAY 57 OF 90

Date: _____

Morning Review

In 34-days I will: _____

My #1 focus today: _____

I'm grateful for: _____

SUCCESS LIST
3 THINGS I MUST DO TODAY
Do the least desired task first!

◊ _____

◊ _____

◊ _____

◆◆◆◆ OTHER TO-DO'S ◆◆◆◆

◊ _____
◊ _____
◊ _____
◊ _____

◆◆◆◆ TASKS TO DELEGATE ◆◆◆◆

◊ _____
◊ _____
◊ _____

◆◆◆◆ HABITS ◆◆◆◆

◊ Visualized My Goal
◊ Exercised
◊ 8 Glasses of Water

♡ ♡ ♡ ♡ ♡ ♡ ♡ ♡

◊ _____
◊ _____
◊ _____

SCHEDULE

4:00	
4:30	
5:00	
5:30	
6:00	
6:30	
7:00	
7:30	
8:00	
8:30	
9:00	
9:30	
10:00	
10:30	
11:00	
11:30	
12:00	
12:30	
1:00	
1:30	
2:00	
2:30	
3:00	
3:30	
4:00	
4:30	
5:00	
5:30	
6:00	
6:30	
7:00	
7:30	
8:00	
8:30	
9:00	
9:30	

End of Day Reflection:

What were your wins today?

What didn't happen & why? How can you fix this moving forward?

Great work today!

Schedule your action plan for tomorrow. →

My Brilliant Ideas or Notes

DAILY ACTION PLAN

DAY 58 OF 90

Date: _____

Morning Review

In 33-days I will: _____
My #1 focus today: _____
I'm grateful for: _____

SUCCESS LIST
3 THINGS I MUST DO TODAY
Do the least desired task first!

◊ _____

◊ _____

◊ _____

❖❖❖❖ OTHER TO-DO'S ❖❖❖❖
◊ _____
◊ _____
◊ _____
◊ _____

❖❖❖❖ TASKS TO DELEGATE ❖❖❖❖
◊ _____
◊ _____
◊ _____

❖❖❖❖ HABITS ❖❖❖❖
◊ Visualized My Goal
◊ Exercised
◊ 8 Glasses of Water
♡ ♡ ♡ ♡ ♡ ♡ ♡ ♡
◊ _____
◊ _____
◊ _____

SCHEDULE

4:00 _____
4:30 _____
5:00 _____
5:30 _____
6:00 _____
6:30 _____
7:00 _____
7:30 _____
8:00 _____
8:30 _____
9:00 _____
9:30 _____
10:00 _____
10:30 _____
11:00 _____
11:30 _____
12:00 _____
12:30 _____
1:00 _____
1:30 _____
2:00 _____
2:30 _____
3:00 _____
3:30 _____
4:00 _____
4:30 _____
5:00 _____
5:30 _____
6:00 _____
6:30 _____
7:00 _____
7:30 _____
8:00 _____
8:30 _____
9:00 _____
9:30 _____

End of Day Reflection:

What were your wins today?

What didn't happen & why? How can you fix this moving forward?

Great work today!

Schedule your action plan for tomorrow. →

My Brilliant Ideas or Notes

DAILY ACTION PLAN

DAY 59 OF 90

Date: _____

Morning Review

In 32-days I will: _____
My #1 focus today: _____
I'm grateful for: _____

SUCCESS LIST
3 THINGS I MUST DO TODAY
Do the least desired task first!

◊ _____

◊ _____

◊ _____

♦♦♦♦♦ OTHER TO-DO'S ♦♦♦♦♦

◊ _____
◊ _____
◊ _____
◊ _____

♦♦♦♦♦ TASKS TO DELEGATE ♦♦♦♦♦

◊ _____
◊ _____
◊ _____

♦♦♦♦♦ HABITS ♦♦♦♦♦

◊ Visualized My Goal
◊ Exercised
◊ 8 Glasses of Water
♡ ♡ ♡ ♡ ♡ ♡ ♡ ♡
◊ _____
◊ _____
◊ _____

SCHEDULE

4:00
4:30
5:00
5:30
6:00
6:30
7:00
7:30
8:00
8:30
9:00
9:30
10:00
10:30
11:00
11:30
12:00
12:30
1:00
1:30
2:00
2:30
3:00
3:30
4:00
4:30
5:00
5:30
6:00
6:30
7:00
7:30
8:00
8:30
9:00
9:30

End of Day Reflection:

What were your wins today?

What didn't happen & why? How can you fix this moving forward?

Great work today!

Schedule your action plan for tomorrow. →

My Brilliant Ideas or Notes

DAILY ACTION PLAN

DAY 60 OF 90

Date: _____

Morning Review

In 31-days I will: _____
My #1 focus today: _____
I'm grateful for: _____

SUCCESS LIST
3 THINGS I MUST DO TODAY
Do the least desired task first!

◇ _____

◇ _____

◇ _____

♦♦♦♦ OTHER TO-DO'S ♦♦♦♦
◇ _____
◇ _____
◇ _____
◇ _____

♦♦♦♦ TASKS TO DELEGATE ♦♦♦♦
◇ _____
◇ _____
◇ _____

♦♦♦♦ HABITS ♦♦♦♦
◇ Visualized My Goal
◇ Exercised
◇ 8 Glasses of Water
♡ ♡ ♡ ♡ ♡ ♡ ♡ ♡
◇ _____
◇ _____
◇ _____

SCHEDULE

4:00	
4:30	
5:00	
5:30	
6:00	
6:30	
7:00	
7:30	
8:00	
8:30	
9:00	
9:30	
10:00	
10:30	
11:00	
11:30	
12:00	
12:30	
1:00	
1:30	
2:00	
2:30	
3:00	
3:30	
4:00	
4:30	
5:00	
5:30	
6:00	
6:30	
7:00	
7:30	
8:00	
8:30	
9:00	
9:30	

End of Day Reflection:

What were your wins today?

What didn't happen & why? How can you fix this moving forward?

Great work today!

Schedule your action plan for tomorrow. →

My Brilliant Ideas or Notes

ROUND SIX: REFLECTION

DID YOU ACHIEVE YOUR MINI GOAL THIS ROUND?

Don't forget to reward yourself!

_____

WHAT SURPRISE ACCOMPLISHMENT DID YOU ACHIEVE?

_____
_____

WHAT DIDN'T HAPPEN OR GO AS PLANNED?

_____
_____
_____

HOW CAN YOU FIX THIS SO IT DOESN'T HAPPEN IN THE FUTURE?

_____
_____
_____

WHAT WAS THE MOST VALUABLE LESSON YOU LEARNED?

_____
_____

GLAMIFY YOUR GOAL

ARE YOU ON TRACK TO ACCOMPLISHING YOUR GOAL?
IF NOT, WHAT CAN YOU DO TO FIX THIS?

Delegate items or find a way to free up more time.

_____
_____
_____
_____
_____

IS ANYTHING LEFT UNFINISHED?
IF SO, HOW DO YOU PLAN TO COMPLETE IT?

_____
_____
_____
_____
_____

WHAT ARE YOU MOST GRATEFUL FOR?

_____
_____
_____
_____
_____

Great job this round girl! Now let's plan Round Seven. →

MINI GOAL PLANNER

ROUND SEVEN: DAYS 61–70

IF I SUCCESSFULLY COMPLETE THIS ROUND, I'LL REWARD MYSELF BY:
_____

If a task has more than one action step, break the task down into smaller steps. This will help increase your focus and make it easier to take action.

MINI GOAL: _____

DATE: From _____ **to** _____

Done?	Tasks/Projects to Complete in Order of Sequence	Delegate Task To:
◊		
◊		
◊		
◊		
◊		
◊		
◊		
◊		
◊		
◊		
◊		
◊		
◊		
◊		

DAILY ACTION PLAN

DAY 61 OF 90

Date: _____

Morning Review

In 30-days I will: _____
My #1 focus today: _____
I'm grateful for: _____

SUCCESS LIST
3 THINGS I MUST DO TODAY
Do the least desired task first!

◊ _____
◊ _____
◊ _____

♦♦♦♦ OTHER TO-DO'S ♦♦♦♦

◊ _____
◊ _____
◊ _____
◊ _____

♦♦♦♦ TASKS TO DELEGATE ♦♦♦♦

◊ _____
◊ _____
◊ _____

♦♦♦♦ HABITS ♦♦♦♦

◊ Visualized My Goal
◊ Exercised
◊ 8 Glasses of Water
♡ ♡ ♡ ♡ ♡ ♡ ♡ ♡

◊ _____
◊ _____
◊ _____

SCHEDULE

4:00 _____
4:30 _____
5:00 _____
5:30 _____
6:00 _____
6:30 _____
7:00 _____
7:30 _____
8:00 _____
8:30 _____
9:00 _____
9:30 _____
10:00 _____
10:30 _____
11:00 _____
11:30 _____
12:00 _____
12:30 _____
1:00 _____
1:30 _____
2:00 _____
2:30 _____
3:00 _____
3:30 _____
4:00 _____
4:30 _____
5:00 _____
5:30 _____
6:00 _____
6:30 _____
7:00 _____
7:30 _____
8:00 _____
8:30 _____
9:00 _____
9:30 _____

End of Day Reflection:

What were your wins today?

What didn't happen & why? How can you fix this moving forward?

Great work today!

Schedule your action plan for tomorrow. →

My Brilliant Ideas or Notes

DAILY ACTION PLAN

DAY 62 OF 90
Date: _____

Morning Review

In 29-days I will: _____
My #1 focus today: _____
I'm grateful for: _____

SUCCESS LIST
3 THINGS I MUST DO TODAY
Do the least desired task first!

◊ _____
◊ _____
◊ _____

♦♦♦♦ OTHER TO-DO'S ♦♦♦♦
◊ _____
◊ _____
◊ _____
◊ _____

♦♦♦♦ TASKS TO DELEGATE ♦♦♦♦
◊ _____
◊ _____
◊ _____

♦♦♦♦ HABITS ♦♦♦♦
◊ Visualized My Goal
◊ Exercised
◊ 8 Glasses of Water
♡ ♡ ♡ ♡ ♡ ♡ ♡ ♡
◊ _____
◊ _____
◊ _____

SCHEDULE

4:00	
4:30	
5:00	
5:30	
6:00	
6:30	
7:00	
7:30	
8:00	
8:30	
9:00	
9:30	
10:00	
10:30	
11:00	
11:30	
12:00	
12:30	
1:00	
1:30	
2:00	
2:30	
3:00	
3:30	
4:00	
4:30	
5:00	
5:30	
6:00	
6:30	
7:00	
7:30	
8:00	
8:30	
9:00	
9:30	

End of Day Reflection:

What were your wins today?

What didn't happen & why? How can you fix this moving forward?

Great work today!

Schedule your action plan for tomorrow. →

My Brilliant Ideas or Notes

DAILY ACTION PLAN

DAY 63 OF 90

Date: _____

Morning Review

In 28-days I will: _____
My #1 focus today: _____
I'm grateful for: _____

SUCCESS LIST
3 THINGS I MUST DO TODAY
Do the least desired task first!

◊ _____
◊ _____
◊ _____

◆◆◆◆ OTHER TO-DO'S ◆◆◆◆

◊ _____
◊ _____
◊ _____
◊ _____

◆◆◆◆ TASKS TO DELEGATE ◆◆◆◆

◊ _____
◊ _____
◊ _____

◆◆◆◆ HABITS ◆◆◆◆

◊ Visualized My Goal
◊ Exercised
◊ 8 Glasses of Water
♡ ♡ ♡ ♡ ♡ ♡ ♡ ♡
◊ _____
◊ _____
◊ _____

SCHEDULE

4:00
4:30
5:00
5:30
6:00
6:30
7:00
7:30
8:00
8:30
9:00
9:30
10:00
10:30
11:00
11:30
12:00
12:30
1:00
1:30
2:00
2:30
3:00
3:30
4:00
4:30
5:00
5:30
6:00
6:30
7:00
7:30
8:00
8:30
9:00
9:30

End of Day Reflection:

What were your wins today?

What didn't happen & why? How can you fix this moving forward?

Great work today!

Schedule your action plan for tomorrow. →

My Brilliant Ideas or Notes

DAILY ACTION PLAN

DAY 64 OF 90

Date: _____

Morning Review

In 27-days I will: _____
My #1 focus today: _____
I'm grateful for: _____

SUCCESS LIST
3 THINGS I MUST DO TODAY
Do the least desired task first!

◊ _____

◊ _____

◊ _____

♦♦♦♦♦ OTHER TO-DO'S ♦♦♦♦♦
◊ _____
◊ _____
◊ _____
◊ _____

♦♦♦♦♦ TASKS TO DELEGATE ♦♦♦♦♦
◊ _____
◊ _____
◊ _____

♦♦♦♦♦ HABITS ♦♦♦♦♦
◊ Visualized My Goal
◊ Exercised
◊ 8 Glasses of Water
♡ ♡ ♡ ♡ ♡ ♡ ♡ ♡
◊ _____
◊ _____
◊ _____

SCHEDULE

4:00	
4:30	
5:00	
5:30	
6:00	
6:30	
7:00	
7:30	
8:00	
8:30	
9:00	
9:30	
10:00	
10:30	
11:00	
11:30	
12:00	
12:30	
1:00	
1:30	
2:00	
2:30	
3:00	
3:30	
4:00	
4:30	
5:00	
5:30	
6:00	
6:30	
7:00	
7:30	
8:00	
8:30	
9:00	
9:30	

End of Day Reflection:

What were your wins today?

What didn't happen & why? How can you fix this moving forward?

Great work today!

Schedule your action plan for tomorrow. →

My Brilliant Ideas or Notes

DAILY ACTION PLAN

DAY 65 OF 90
Date: _____

Morning Review

In 26-days I will: _____
My #1 focus today: _____
I'm grateful for: _____

SUCCESS LIST
3 THINGS I MUST DO TODAY
Do the least desired task first!

◊ _____
◊ _____
◊ _____

✦✦✦✦ OTHER TO-DO'S ✦✦✦✦
◊ _____
◊ _____
◊ _____
◊ _____

✦✦✦✦ TASKS TO DELEGATE ✦✦✦✦
◊ _____
◊ _____
◊ _____

✦✦✦✦ HABITS ✦✦✦✦
◊ Visualized My Goal
◊ Exercised
◊ 8 Glasses of Water
♡ ♡ ♡ ♡ ♡ ♡ ♡ ♡
◊ _____
◊ _____
◊ _____

SCHEDULE
4:00
4:30
5:00
5:30
6:00
6:30
7:00
7:30
8:00
8:30
9:00
9:30
10:00
10:30
11:00
11:30
12:00
12:30
1:00
1:30
2:00
2:30
3:00
3:30
4:00
4:30
5:00
5:30
6:00
6:30
7:00
7:30
8:00
8:30
9:00
9:30

End of Day Reflection:

What were your wins today?

What didn't happen & why? How can you fix this moving forward?

Great work today!

Schedule your action plan for tomorrow. →

My Brilliant Ideas or Notes

DAILY ACTION PLAN

DAY 66 OF 90

Date: _____

Morning Review

In 25-days I will: _____
My #1 focus today: _____
I'm grateful for: _____

SUCCESS LIST
3 THINGS I MUST DO TODAY
Do the least desired task first!

◊ _____
◊ _____
◊ _____

♦♦♦♦♦ OTHER TO-DO'S ♦♦♦♦♦
◊ _____
◊ _____
◊ _____
◊ _____

♦♦♦♦♦ TASKS TO DELEGATE ♦♦♦♦♦
◊ _____
◊ _____
◊ _____

♦♦♦♦ HABITS ♦♦♦♦
◊ Visualized My Goal
◊ Exercised
◊ 8 Glasses of Water
♡ ♡ ♡ ♡ ♡ ♡ ♡ ♡
◊ _____
◊ _____
◊ _____

SCHEDULE

4:00
4:30
5:00
5:30
6:00
6:30
7:00
7:30
8:00
8:30
9:00
9:30
10:00
10:30
11:00
11:30
12:00
12:30
1:00
1:30
2:00
2:30
3:00
3:30
4:00
4:30
5:00
5:30
6:00
6:30
7:00
7:30
8:00
8:30
9:00
9:30

End of Day Reflection:

What were your wins today?

What didn't happen & why? How can you fix this moving forward?

Great work today!

Schedule your action plan for tomorrow. →

My Brilliant Ideas or Notes

DAILY ACTION PLAN

DAY 67 OF 90

Date: _____

Morning Review

In 24-days I will: _____
My #1 focus today: _____
I'm grateful for: _____

SUCCESS LIST
3 THINGS I MUST DO TODAY
Do the least desired task first!

◇ _____

◇ _____

◇ _____

♦♦♦♦♦ OTHER TO-DO'S ♦♦♦♦♦
◇ _____
◇ _____
◇ _____
◇ _____

♦♦♦♦♦ TASKS TO DELEGATE ♦♦♦♦♦
◇ _____
◇ _____
◇ _____

♦♦♦♦♦ HABITS ♦♦♦♦♦
◇ Visualized My Goal
◇ Exercised
◇ 8 Glasses of Water
♡♡♡♡♡♡♡♡
◇ _____
◇ _____
◇ _____

SCHEDULE
4:00	
4:30	
5:00	
5:30	
6:00	
6:30	
7:00	
7:30	
8:00	
8:30	
9:00	
9:30	
10:00	
10:30	
11:00	
11:30	
12:00	
12:30	
1:00	
1:30	
2:00	
2:30	
3:00	
3:30	
4:00	
4:30	
5:00	
5:30	
6:00	
6:30	
7:00	
7:30	
8:00	
8:30	
9:00	
9:30	

End of Day Reflection:

What were your wins today?

What didn't happen & why? How can you fix this moving forward?

Great work today!

Schedule your action plan for tomorrow. →

My Brilliant Ideas or Notes

DAILY ACTION PLAN

DAY 68 OF 90

Date: _____

Morning Review

In 23-days I will: _____

My #1 focus today: _____

I'm grateful for: _____

SUCCESS LIST
3 THINGS I MUST DO TODAY
Do the least desired task first!

◊ _____

◊ _____

◊ _____

♦♦♦♦♦ OTHER TO-DO'S ♦♦♦♦♦

◊ _____
◊ _____
◊ _____
◊ _____

♦♦♦♦♦ TASKS TO DELEGATE ♦♦♦♦♦

◊ _____
◊ _____
◊ _____

♦♦♦♦ HABITS ♦♦♦♦

◊ Visualized My Goal
◊ Exercised
◊ 8 Glasses of Water
♡ ♡ ♡ ♡ ♡ ♡ ♡ ♡

◊ _____
◊ _____
◊ _____

SCHEDULE

4:00	
4:30	
5:00	
5:30	
6:00	
6:30	
7:00	
7:30	
8:00	
8:30	
9:00	
9:30	
10:00	
10:30	
11:00	
11:30	
12:00	
12:30	
1:00	
1:30	
2:00	
2:30	
3:00	
3:30	
4:00	
4:30	
5:00	
5:30	
6:00	
6:30	
7:00	
7:30	
8:00	
8:30	
9:00	
9:30	

End of Day Reflection:

What were your wins today?

What didn't happen & why? How can you fix this moving forward?

Great work today!

Schedule your action plan for tomorrow. →

My Brilliant Ideas or Notes

DAILY ACTION PLAN

DAY 69 OF 90

Date: _____

Morning Review

In 22-days I will: _____
My #1 focus today: _____
I'm grateful for: _____

SUCCESS LIST
3 THINGS I MUST DO TODAY
Do the least desired task first!

◊ _____

◊ _____

◊ _____

◆◆◆◆ OTHER TO-DO'S ◆◆◆◆
◊ _____
◊ _____
◊ _____
◊ _____

◆◆◆◆ TASKS TO DELEGATE ◆◆◆◆
◊ _____
◊ _____
◊ _____

◆◆◆◆ HABITS ◆◆◆◆
◊ Visualized My Goal
◊ Exercised
◊ 8 Glasses of Water
♡ ♡ ♡ ♡ ♡ ♡ ♡ ♡

◊ _____
◊ _____
◊ _____

SCHEDULE

4:00	
4:30	
5:00	
5:30	
6:00	
6:30	
7:00	
7:30	
8:00	
8:30	
9:00	
9:30	
10:00	
10:30	
11:00	
11:30	
12:00	
12:30	
1:00	
1:30	
2:00	
2:30	
3:00	
3:30	
4:00	
4:30	
5:00	
5:30	
6:00	
6:30	
7:00	
7:30	
8:00	
8:30	
9:00	
9:30	

End of Day Reflection:

What were your wins today?

What didn't happen & why? How can you fix this moving forward?

Great work today!

Schedule your action plan for tomorrow. →

My Brilliant Ideas or Notes

DAILY ACTION PLAN

DAY 70 OF 90

Date: _____

Morning Review

In 21-days I will: _____
My #1 focus today: _____
I'm grateful for: _____

SUCCESS LIST
3 THINGS I MUST DO TODAY
Do the least desired task first!

◊ _____
◊ _____
◊ _____

♦♦♦♦♦ OTHER TO-DO'S ♦♦♦♦♦
◊ _____
◊ _____
◊ _____
◊ _____

♦♦♦♦♦ TASKS TO DELEGATE ♦♦♦♦♦
◊ _____
◊ _____
◊ _____

♦♦♦♦♦ HABITS ♦♦♦♦♦
◊ Visualized My Goal
◊ Exercised
◊ 8 Glasses of Water
♡ ♡ ♡ ♡ ♡ ♡ ♡ ♡
◊ _____
◊ _____
◊ _____

SCHEDULE

4:00
4:30
5:00
5:30
6:00
6:30
7:00
7:30
8:00
8:30
9:00
9:30
10:00
10:30
11:00
11:30
12:00
12:30
1:00
1:30
2:00
2:30
3:00
3:30
4:00
4:30
5:00
5:30
6:00
6:30
7:00
7:30
8:00
8:30
9:00
9:30

End of Day Reflection:

What were your wins today?

What didn't happen & why? How can you fix this moving forward?

Great work today!

Schedule your action plan for tomorrow. →

My Brilliant Ideas or Notes

ROUND SEVEN: REFLECTION

DID YOU ACHIEVE YOUR MINI GOAL THIS ROUND?

Don't forget to reward yourself!

_____

WHAT SURPRISE ACCOMPLISHMENT DID YOU ACHIEVE?

_____
_____

WHAT DIDN'T HAPPEN OR GO AS PLANNED?

_____
_____
_____

HOW CAN YOU FIX THIS SO IT DOESN'T HAPPEN IN THE FUTURE?

_____
_____
_____

WHAT WAS THE MOST VALUABLE LESSON YOU LEARNED?

_____
_____

ARE YOU ON TRACK TO ACCOMPLISHING YOUR GOAL?
IF NOT, WHAT CAN YOU DO TO FIX THIS?

Delegate items or find a way to free up more time.

_____
_____
_____
_____
_____

IS ANYTHING LEFT UNFINISHED?
IF SO, HOW DO YOU PLAN TO COMPLETE IT?

_____
_____
_____
_____
_____

WHAT ARE YOU MOST GRATEFUL FOR?

_____
_____
_____
_____
_____

Great job this round girl! Now let's plan Round Eight. →

MINI GOAL PLANNER

ROUND EIGHT: DAYS 71–80

IF I SUCCESSFULLY COMPLETE THIS ROUND, I'LL REWARD MYSELF BY:
_____

◆ If a task has more than one action step, break the task down into smaller steps. This will help increase your focus and make it easier to take action.

MINI GOAL: _____

DATE: From _____ **to** _____

Done?	Tasks/Projects to Complete in Order of Sequence	Delegate Task To:
◇		
◇		
◇		
◇		
◇		
◇		
◇		
◇		
◇		
◇		
◇		
◇		
◇		
◇		

DAILY ACTION PLAN

DAY 71 OF 90

Date: _____

Morning Review

In 20-days I will: _____
My #1 focus today: _____
I'm grateful for: _____

SUCCESS LIST
3 THINGS I MUST DO TODAY
Do the least desired task first!

◊ _____

◊ _____

◊ _____

♦♦♦♦ OTHER TO-DO'S ♦♦♦♦

◊ _____
◊ _____
◊ _____
◊ _____

♦♦♦♦ TASKS TO DELEGATE ♦♦♦♦

◊ _____
◊ _____
◊ _____

♦♦♦♦ HABITS ♦♦♦♦

◊ Visualized My Goal
◊ Exercised
◊ 8 Glasses of Water
♡ ♡ ♡ ♡ ♡ ♡ ♡ ♡
◊ _____
◊ _____
◊ _____

SCHEDULE

4:00	
4:30	
5:00	
5:30	
6:00	
6:30	
7:00	
7:30	
8:00	
8:30	
9:00	
9:30	
10:00	
10:30	
11:00	
11:30	
12:00	
12:30	
1:00	
1:30	
2:00	
2:30	
3:00	
3:30	
4:00	
4:30	
5:00	
5:30	
6:00	
6:30	
7:00	
7:30	
8:00	
8:30	
9:00	
9:30	

End of Day Reflection:

What were your wins today?

What didn't happen & why? How can you fix this moving forward?

Great work today!

Schedule your action plan for tomorrow. →

My Brilliant Ideas or Notes

DAILY ACTION PLAN

DAY 72 OF 90
Date: _____

Morning Review

In 19-days I will: _____
My #1 focus today: _____
I'm grateful for: _____

SUCCESS LIST
3 THINGS I MUST DO TODAY
Do the least desired task first!

◊ _____
◊ _____
◊ _____

♦♦♦♦♦ OTHER TO-DO'S ♦♦♦♦♦

◊ _____
◊ _____
◊ _____
◊ _____

♦♦♦♦♦ TASKS TO DELEGATE ♦♦♦♦♦

◊ _____
◊ _____
◊ _____

♦♦♦♦♦ HABITS ♦♦♦♦♦

◊ Visualized My Goal
◊ Exercised
◊ 8 Glasses of Water
♡ ♡ ♡ ♡ ♡ ♡ ♡ ♡

◊ _____
◊ _____
◊ _____

SCHEDULE

4:00	
4:30	
5:00	
5:30	
6:00	
6:30	
7:00	
7:30	
8:00	
8:30	
9:00	
9:30	
10:00	
10:30	
11:00	
11:30	
12:00	
12:30	
1:00	
1:30	
2:00	
2:30	
3:00	
3:30	
4:00	
4:30	
5:00	
5:30	
6:00	
6:30	
7:00	
7:30	
8:00	
8:30	
9:00	
9:30	

End of Day Reflection:

What were your wins today?

What didn't happen & why? How can you fix this moving forward?

Great work today!

Schedule your action plan for tomorrow. →

My Brilliant Ideas or Notes

DAILY ACTION PLAN

DAY 73 OF 90

Date: _____

Morning Review

In 18-days I will: _____
My #1 focus today: _____
I'm grateful for: _____

SUCCESS LIST
3 THINGS I MUST DO TODAY
Do the least desired task first!

◊ _____

◊ _____

◊ _____

♦♦♦♦♦ OTHER TO-DO'S ♦♦♦♦♦

◊ _____
◊ _____
◊ _____
◊ _____

♦♦♦♦♦ TASKS TO DELEGATE ♦♦♦♦♦

◊ _____
◊ _____
◊ _____

♦♦♦♦♦ HABITS ♦♦♦♦♦

◊ Visualized My Goal
◊ Exercised
◊ 8 Glasses of Water
♡ ♡ ♡ ♡ ♡ ♡ ♡ ♡

◊ _____
◊ _____
◊ _____

SCHEDULE

4:00
4:30
5:00
5:30
6:00
6:30
7:00
7:30
8:00
8:30
9:00
9:30
10:00
10:30
11:00
11:30
12:00
12:30
1:00
1:30
2:00
2:30
3:00
3:30
4:00
4:30
5:00
5:30
6:00
6:30
7:00
7:30
8:00
8:30
9:00
9:30

End of Day Reflection:

What were your wins today?

What didn't happen & why? How can you fix this moving forward?

Great work today!

Schedule your action plan for tomorrow. →

My Brilliant Ideas or Notes

DAILY ACTION PLAN

DAY 74 OF 90

Date: _____

Morning Review

In 17-days I will: _____
My #1 focus today: _____
I'm grateful for: _____

SUCCESS LIST
3 THINGS I MUST DO TODAY
Do the least desired task first!

◊ _____

◊ _____

◊ _____

♦♦♦♦ OTHER TO-DO'S ♦♦♦♦
◊ _____
◊ _____
◊ _____
◊ _____

♦♦♦♦ TASKS TO DELEGATE ♦♦♦♦
◊ _____
◊ _____
◊ _____

♦♦♦♦ HABITS ♦♦♦♦
◊ Visualized My Goal
◊ Exercised
◊ 8 Glasses of Water
♡ ♡ ♡ ♡ ♡ ♡ ♡ ♡
◊ _____
◊ _____
◊ _____

SCHEDULE
4:00	
4:30	
5:00	
5:30	
6:00	
6:30	
7:00	
7:30	
8:00	
8:30	
9:00	
9:30	
10:00	
10:30	
11:00	
11:30	
12:00	
12:30	
1:00	
1:30	
2:00	
2:30	
3:00	
3:30	
4:00	
4:30	
5:00	
5:30	
6:00	
6:30	
7:00	
7:30	
8:00	
8:30	
9:00	
9:30	

End of Day Reflection:

What were your wins today?

What didn't happen & why? How can you fix this moving forward?

Great work today!

Schedule your action plan for tomorrow. →

My Brilliant Ideas or Notes

DAILY ACTION PLAN

DAY 75 OF 90

Date: _____

Morning Review

In 16-days I will: _____
My #1 focus today: _____
I'm grateful for: _____

SUCCESS LIST
3 THINGS I MUST DO TODAY
Do the least desired task first!

◊ _____

◊ _____

◊ _____

♦♦♦♦♦ OTHER TO-DO'S ♦♦♦♦♦

◊ _____
◊ _____
◊ _____
◊ _____

♦♦♦♦♦ TASKS TO DELEGATE ♦♦♦♦♦

◊ _____
◊ _____
◊ _____

♦♦♦♦♦ HABITS ♦♦♦♦♦

◊ Visualized My Goal
◊ Exercised
◊ 8 Glasses of Water
♡ ♡ ♡ ♡ ♡ ♡ ♡ ♡
◊ _____
◊ _____
◊ _____

SCHEDULE

4:00	
4:30	
5:00	
5:30	
6:00	
6:30	
7:00	
7:30	
8:00	
8:30	
9:00	
9:30	
10:00	
10:30	
11:00	
11:30	
12:00	
12:30	
1:00	
1:30	
2:00	
2:30	
3:00	
3:30	
4:00	
4:30	
5:00	
5:30	
6:00	
6:30	
7:00	
7:30	
8:00	
8:30	
9:00	
9:30	

End of Day Reflection:

What were your wins today?

What didn't happen & why? How can you fix this moving forward?

Great work today!

Schedule your action plan for tomorrow. →

My Brilliant Ideas or Notes

DAILY ACTION PLAN

DAY 76 OF 90
Date: _____

Morning Review

In 15-days I will: _____
My #1 focus today: _____
I'm grateful for: _____

SUCCESS LIST
3 THINGS I MUST DO TODAY
Do the least desired task first!

◊ _____
◊ _____
◊ _____

✦✦✦✦ OTHER TO-DO'S ✦✦✦✦
◊ _____
◊ _____
◊ _____
◊ _____

✦✦✦✦ TASKS TO DELEGATE ✦✦✦✦
◊ _____
◊ _____
◊ _____

✦✦✦✦ HABITS ✦✦✦✦
◊ Visualized My Goal
◊ Exercised
◊ 8 Glasses of Water
♡ ♡ ♡ ♡ ♡ ♡ ♡ ♡
◊ _____
◊ _____
◊ _____

SCHEDULE

4:00	
4:30	
5:00	
5:30	
6:00	
6:30	
7:00	
7:30	
8:00	
8:30	
9:00	
9:30	
10:00	
10:30	
11:00	
11:30	
12:00	
12:30	
1:00	
1:30	
2:00	
2:30	
3:00	
3:30	
4:00	
4:30	
5:00	
5:30	
6:00	
6:30	
7:00	
7:30	
8:00	
8:30	
9:00	
9:30	

End of Day Reflection:

What were your wins today?

What didn't happen & why? How can you fix this moving forward?

Great work today!

Schedule your action plan for tomorrow. →

My Brilliant Ideas or Notes

DAILY ACTION PLAN

DAY 77 OF 90

Date: _____

Morning Review

In 14-days I will: _____
My #1 focus today: _____
I'm grateful for: _____

SUCCESS LIST
3 THINGS I MUST DO TODAY
Do the least desired task first!

◇ _____

◇ _____

◇ _____

◆◆◆◆◆ OTHER TO-DO'S ◆◆◆◆◆

◇ _____
◇ _____
◇ _____
◇ _____

◆◆◆◆◆ TASKS TO DELEGATE ◆◆◆◆◆

◇ _____
◇ _____
◇ _____

◆◆◆◆◆ HABITS ◆◆◆◆◆

◇ Visualized My Goal
◇ Exercised
◇ 8 Glasses of Water
♡ ♡ ♡ ♡ ♡ ♡ ♡ ♡

◇ _____
◇ _____
◇ _____

SCHEDULE

4:00	
4:30	
5:00	
5:30	
6:00	
6:30	
7:00	
7:30	
8:00	
8:30	
9:00	
9:30	
10:00	
10:30	
11:00	
11:30	
12:00	
12:30	
1:00	
1:30	
2:00	
2:30	
3:00	
3:30	
4:00	
4:30	
5:00	
5:30	
6:00	
6:30	
7:00	
7:30	
8:00	
8:30	
9:00	
9:30	

End of Day Reflection:

What were your wins today?

What didn't happen & why? How can you fix this moving forward?

Great work today!

Schedule your action plan for tomorrow. →

My Brilliant Ideas or Notes

DAILY ACTION PLAN

DAY 78 OF 90
Date: _____

Morning Review

In 13-days I will: _____
My #1 focus today: _____
I'm grateful for: _____

SUCCESS LIST
3 THINGS I MUST DO TODAY
Do the least desired task first!

◊ _____
◊ _____
◊ _____

♦♦♦♦♦ OTHER TO-DO'S ♦♦♦♦♦
◊ _____
◊ _____
◊ _____
◊ _____

♦♦♦♦♦ TASKS TO DELEGATE ♦♦♦♦♦
◊ _____
◊ _____
◊ _____

♦♦♦♦♦ HABITS ♦♦♦♦♦
◊ Visualized My Goal
◊ Exercised
◊ 8 Glasses of Water
♡ ♡ ♡ ♡ ♡ ♡ ♡ ♡
◊ _____
◊ _____
◊ _____

SCHEDULE

4:00	
4:30	
5:00	
5:30	
6:00	
6:30	
7:00	
7:30	
8:00	
8:30	
9:00	
9:30	
10:00	
10:30	
11:00	
11:30	
12:00	
12:30	
1:00	
1:30	
2:00	
2:30	
3:00	
3:30	
4:00	
4:30	
5:00	
5:30	
6:00	
6:30	
7:00	
7:30	
8:00	
8:30	
9:00	
9:30	

End of Day Reflection:

What were your wins today?

What didn't happen & why? How can you fix this moving forward?

Great work today!

Schedule your action plan for tomorrow. →

My Brilliant Ideas or Notes

DAILY ACTION PLAN

DAY 79 OF 90

Date: _____

Morning Review

In 12-days I will: _____
My #1 focus today: _____
I'm grateful for: _____

SUCCESS LIST
3 THINGS I MUST DO TODAY
Do the least desired task first!

◊ _____

◊ _____

◊ _____

♦♦♦♦♦ OTHER TO-DO'S ♦♦♦♦♦
◊ _____
◊ _____
◊ _____
◊ _____

♦♦♦♦♦ TASKS TO DELEGATE ♦♦♦♦♦
◊ _____
◊ _____
◊ _____

♦♦♦♦♦ HABITS ♦♦♦♦♦
◊ Visualized My Goal
◊ Exercised
◊ 8 Glasses of Water
♡ ♡ ♡ ♡ ♡ ♡ ♡ ♡
◊ _____
◊ _____
◊ _____

SCHEDULE

4:00	
4:30	
5:00	
5:30	
6:00	
6:30	
7:00	
7:30	
8:00	
8:30	
9:00	
9:30	
10:00	
10:30	
11:00	
11:30	
12:00	
12:30	
1:00	
1:30	
2:00	
2:30	
3:00	
3:30	
4:00	
4:30	
5:00	
5:30	
6:00	
6:30	
7:00	
7:30	
8:00	
8:30	
9:00	
9:30	

End of Day Reflection:

What were your wins today?

What didn't happen & why? How can you fix this moving forward?

Great work today!

Schedule your action plan for tomorrow. →

My Brilliant Ideas or Notes

DAILY ACTION PLAN

DAY 80 OF 90

Date: _____

Morning Review

In 11-days I will: _____
My #1 focus today: _____
I'm grateful for: _____

SUCCESS LIST
3 THINGS I MUST DO TODAY
Do the least desired task first!

◊ _____

◊ _____

◊ _____

◆◆◆◆◆ OTHER TO-DO'S ◆◆◆◆◆

◊ _____
◊ _____
◊ _____
◊ _____

◆◆◆◆◆ TASKS TO DELEGATE ◆◆◆◆◆

◊ _____
◊ _____
◊ _____

◆◆◆◆◆ HABITS ◆◆◆◆◆

◊ Visualized My Goal
◊ Exercised
◊ 8 Glasses of Water
♡ ♡ ♡ ♡ ♡ ♡ ♡ ♡

◊ _____
◊ _____
◊ _____

SCHEDULE

4:00	
4:30	
5:00	
5:30	
6:00	
6:30	
7:00	
7:30	
8:00	
8:30	
9:00	
9:30	
10:00	
10:30	
11:00	
11:30	
12:00	
12:30	
1:00	
1:30	
2:00	
2:30	
3:00	
3:30	
4:00	
4:30	
5:00	
5:30	
6:00	
6:30	
7:00	
7:30	
8:00	
8:30	
9:00	
9:30	

End of Day Reflection:

What were your wins today?

What didn't happen & why? How can you fix this moving forward?

Great work today!

Schedule your action plan for tomorrow. →

My Brilliant Ideas or Notes

ROUND EIGHT: REFLECTION

DID YOU ACHIEVE YOUR MINI GOAL THIS ROUND?
Don't forget to reward yourself!

_____

WHAT SURPRISE ACCOMPLISHMENT DID YOU ACHIEVE?
_____
_____

WHAT DIDN'T HAPPEN OR GO AS PLANNED?
_____
_____
_____

HOW CAN YOU FIX THIS SO IT DOESN'T HAPPEN IN THE FUTURE?
_____
_____
_____

WHAT WAS THE MOST VALUABLE LESSON YOU LEARNED?
_____
_____

ARE YOU ON TRACK TO ACCOMPLISHING YOUR GOAL?
IF NOT, WHAT CAN YOU DO TO FIX THIS?

Delegate items or find a way to free up more time.

_____
_____
_____
_____
_____

IS ANYTHING LEFT UNFINISHED?
IF SO, HOW DO YOU PLAN TO COMPLETE IT?

_____
_____
_____
_____
_____

WHAT ARE YOU MOST GRATEFUL FOR?

_____
_____
_____
_____
_____

Great job this round girl! Now let's plan Round Nine. →

MINI GOAL PLANNER

ROUND NINE: DAYS 81–90

IF I SUCCESSFULLY COMPLETE THIS ROUND, I'LL REWARD MYSELF BY:

_____

◆ If a task has more than one action step, break the task down into smaller steps. This will help increase your focus and make it easier to take action.

MINI GOAL: _____

DATE: From _____ **to** _____

Done?	Tasks/Projects to Complete in Order of Sequence	Delegate Task To:
◇		
◇		
◇		
◇		
◇		
◇		
◇		
◇		
◇		
◇		
◇		
◇		
◇		
◇		

DAILY ACTION PLAN

DAY 81 OF 90

Date: _____

Morning Review

In 10-days I will: _____
My #1 focus today: _____
I'm grateful for: _____

SUCCESS LIST
3 THINGS I MUST DO TODAY
Do the least desired task first!

◊ _____

◊ _____

◊ _____

♦♦♦♦ OTHER TO-DO'S ♦♦♦♦
◊ _____
◊ _____
◊ _____
◊ _____

♦♦♦♦ TASKS TO DELEGATE ♦♦♦♦
◊ _____
◊ _____
◊ _____

♦♦♦♦ HABITS ♦♦♦♦
◊ Visualized My Goal
◊ Exercised
◊ 8 Glasses of Water
♡ ♡ ♡ ♡ ♡ ♡ ♡ ♡
◊ _____
◊ _____
◊ _____

SCHEDULE

4:00
4:30
5:00
5:30
6:00
6:30
7:00
7:30
8:00
8:30
9:00
9:30
10:00
10:30
11:00
11:30
12:00
12:30
1:00
1:30
2:00
2:30
3:00
3:30
4:00
4:30
5:00
5:30
6:00
6:30
7:00
7:30
8:00
8:30
9:00
9:30

End of Day Reflection:

What were your wins today?

What didn't happen & why? How can you fix this moving forward?

Great work today!

Schedule your action plan for tomorrow. →

My Brilliant Ideas or Notes

DAILY ACTION PLAN

DAY 82 OF 90

Date: _____

Morning Review

In 9-days I will: _____
My #1 focus today: _____
I'm grateful for: _____

SUCCESS LIST
3 THINGS I MUST DO TODAY
Do the least desired task first!

◊ _____

◊ _____

◊ _____

✦✦✦✦✦ OTHER TO-DO'S ✦✦✦✦✦
◊ _____
◊ _____
◊ _____
◊ _____

✦✦✦✦✦ TASKS TO DELEGATE ✦✦✦✦✦
◊ _____
◊ _____
◊ _____

✦✦✦✦✦ HABITS ✦✦✦✦✦
◊ Visualized My Goal
◊ Exercised
◊ 8 Glasses of Water
♡ ♡ ♡ ♡ ♡ ♡ ♡ ♡
◊ _____
◊ _____
◊ _____

SCHEDULE

4:00	
4:30	
5:00	
5:30	
6:00	
6:30	
7:00	
7:30	
8:00	
8:30	
9:00	
9:30	
10:00	
10:30	
11:00	
11:30	
12:00	
12:30	
1:00	
1:30	
2:00	
2:30	
3:00	
3:30	
4:00	
4:30	
5:00	
5:30	
6:00	
6:30	
7:00	
7:30	
8:00	
8:30	
9:00	
9:30	

End of Day Reflection:

What were your wins today?

What didn't happen & why? How can you fix this moving forward?

Great work today!

Schedule your action plan for tomorrow. →

My Brilliant Ideas or Notes

DAILY ACTION PLAN

DAY 83 OF 90
Date: _____

Morning Review

In 8-days I will: _____
My #1 focus today: _____
I'm grateful for: _____

SUCCESS LIST
3 THINGS I MUST DO TODAY
Do the least desired task first!

◊ _____

◊ _____

◊ _____

♦♦♦♦ OTHER TO-DO'S ♦♦♦♦

◊ _____
◊ _____
◊ _____
◊ _____

♦♦♦♦ TASKS TO DELEGATE ♦♦♦♦

◊ _____
◊ _____
◊ _____

♦♦♦♦ HABITS ♦♦♦♦

◊ Visualized My Goal
◊ Exercised
◊ 8 Glasses of Water
♡ ♡ ♡ ♡ ♡ ♡ ♡ ♡
◊ _____
◊ _____
◊ _____

SCHEDULE

4:00	
4:30	
5:00	
5:30	
6:00	
6:30	
7:00	
7:30	
8:00	
8:30	
9:00	
9:30	
10:00	
10:30	
11:00	
11:30	
12:00	
12:30	
1:00	
1:30	
2:00	
2:30	
3:00	
3:30	
4:00	
4:30	
5:00	
5:30	
6:00	
6:30	
7:00	
7:30	
8:00	
8:30	
9:00	
9:30	

End of Day Reflection:

What were your wins today?

What didn't happen & why? How can you fix this moving forward?

Great work today!

Schedule your action plan for tomorrow. →

My Brilliant Ideas or Notes

DAILY ACTION PLAN

DAY 84 OF 90

Date: _____

Morning Review

In 7-days I will: _____
My #1 focus today: _____
I'm grateful for: _____

SUCCESS LIST
3 THINGS I MUST DO TODAY
Do the least desired task first!

◇ _____

◇ _____

◇ _____

♦♦♦♦♦ OTHER TO-DO'S ♦♦♦♦♦
◇ _____
◇ _____
◇ _____
◇ _____

♦♦♦♦♦ TASKS TO DELEGATE ♦♦♦♦♦
◇ _____
◇ _____
◇ _____

♦♦♦♦♦ HABITS ♦♦♦♦♦
◇ Visualized My Goal
◇ Exercised
◇ 8 Glasses of Water
♡ ♡ ♡ ♡ ♡ ♡ ♡ ♡
◇ _____
◇ _____
◇ _____

SCHEDULE

4:00
4:30
5:00
5:30
6:00
6:30
7:00
7:30
8:00
8:30
9:00
9:30
10:00
10:30
11:00
11:30
12:00
12:30
1:00
1:30
2:00
2:30
3:00
3:30
4:00
4:30
5:00
5:30
6:00
6:30
7:00
7:30
8:00
8:30
9:00
9:30

End of Day Reflection:

What were your wins today?

What didn't happen & why? How can you fix this moving forward?

Great work today!

Schedule your action plan for tomorrow. →

My Brilliant Ideas or Notes

DAILY ACTION PLAN

DAY 85 OF 90

Date: _____

Morning Review

In 6-days I will: _____
My #1 focus today: _____
I'm grateful for: _____

SUCCESS LIST
3 THINGS I MUST DO TODAY
Do the least desired task first!

◇ _____

◇ _____

◇ _____

♦♦♦♦ OTHER TO-DO'S ♦♦♦♦

◇ _____
◇ _____
◇ _____
◇ _____

♦♦♦♦ TASKS TO DELEGATE ♦♦♦♦

◇ _____
◇ _____
◇ _____

♦♦♦♦ HABITS ♦♦♦♦

◇ Visualized My Goal
◇ Exercised
◇ 8 Glasses of Water
♡ ♡ ♡ ♡ ♡ ♡ ♡ ♡
◇ _____
◇ _____
◇ _____

SCHEDULE

4:00	
4:30	
5:00	
5:30	
6:00	
6:30	
7:00	
7:30	
8:00	
8:30	
9:00	
9:30	
10:00	
10:30	
11:00	
11:30	
12:00	
12:30	
1:00	
1:30	
2:00	
2:30	
3:00	
3:30	
4:00	
4:30	
5:00	
5:30	
6:00	
6:30	
7:00	
7:30	
8:00	
8:30	
9:00	
9:30	

End of Day Reflection:

What were your wins today?

What didn't happen & why? How can you fix this moving forward?

Great work today!

Schedule your action plan for tomorrow. →

My Brilliant Ideas or Notes

DAILY ACTION PLAN

DAY 86 OF 90

Date: _____

Morning Review

In 5-days I will: _____
My #1 focus today: _____
I'm grateful for: _____

SUCCESS LIST
3 THINGS I MUST DO TODAY
Do the least desired task first!

◊ _____

◊ _____

◊ _____

✦✦✦✦✦ OTHER TO-DO'S ✦✦✦✦✦
◊ _____
◊ _____
◊ _____
◊ _____

✦✦✦✦✦ TASKS TO DELEGATE ✦✦✦✦✦
◊ _____
◊ _____
◊ _____

✦✦✦✦✦ HABITS ✦✦✦✦✦
◊ Visualized My Goal
◊ Exercised
◊ 8 Glasses of Water
♡ ♡ ♡ ♡ ♡ ♡ ♡ ♡
◊ _____
◊ _____
◊ _____

SCHEDULE

4:00	
4:30	
5:00	
5:30	
6:00	
6:30	
7:00	
7:30	
8:00	
8:30	
9:00	
9:30	
10:00	
10:30	
11:00	
11:30	
12:00	
12:30	
1:00	
1:30	
2:00	
2:30	
3:00	
3:30	
4:00	
4:30	
5:00	
5:30	
6:00	
6:30	
7:00	
7:30	
8:00	
8:30	
9:00	
9:30	

End of Day Reflection:

What were your wins today?

What didn't happen & why? How can you fix this moving forward?

Great work today!

Schedule your action plan for tomorrow. →

My Brilliant Ideas or Notes

DAILY ACTION PLAN

DAY 87 OF 90

Date: _____

Morning Review

In 4-days I will: _____
My #1 focus today: _____
I'm grateful for: _____

SUCCESS LIST
3 THINGS I MUST DO TODAY
Do the least desired task first!

◊ _____

◊ _____

◊ _____

♦♦♦♦ OTHER TO-DO'S ♦♦♦♦
◊ _____
◊ _____
◊ _____
◊ _____

♦♦♦♦ TASKS TO DELEGATE ♦♦♦♦
◊ _____
◊ _____
◊ _____

♦♦♦♦ HABITS ♦♦♦♦
◊ Visualized My Goal
◊ Exercised
◊ 8 Glasses of Water
♡ ♡ ♡ ♡ ♡ ♡ ♡ ♡
◊ _____
◊ _____
◊ _____

SCHEDULE

4:00	
4:30	
5:00	
5:30	
6:00	
6:30	
7:00	
7:30	
8:00	
8:30	
9:00	
9:30	
10:00	
10:30	
11:00	
11:30	
12:00	
12:30	
1:00	
1:30	
2:00	
2:30	
3:00	
3:30	
4:00	
4:30	
5:00	
5:30	
6:00	
6:30	
7:00	
7:30	
8:00	
8:30	
9:00	
9:30	

End of Day Reflection:

What were your wins today?

What didn't happen & why? How can you fix this moving forward?

Great work today!

Schedule your action plan for tomorrow. →

My Brilliant Ideas or Notes

DAILY ACTION PLAN

DAY 88 OF 90

Date: _____

Morning Review

In 3-days I will: _____
My #1 focus today: _____
I'm grateful for: _____

SUCCESS LIST
3 THINGS I MUST DO TODAY
Do the least desired task first!

◊ _____

◊ _____

◊ _____

♦♦♦♦♦ OTHER TO-DO'S ♦♦♦♦♦
◊ _____
◊ _____
◊ _____
◊ _____

♦♦♦♦♦ TASKS TO DELEGATE ♦♦♦♦♦
◊ _____
◊ _____
◊ _____

♦♦♦♦♦ HABITS ♦♦♦♦♦
◊ Visualized My Goal
◊ Exercised
◊ 8 Glasses of Water
♡ ♡ ♡ ♡ ♡ ♡ ♡ ♡
◊ _____
◊ _____
◊ _____

SCHEDULE
4:00	
4:30	
5:00	
5:30	
6:00	
6:30	
7:00	
7:30	
8:00	
8:30	
9:00	
9:30	
10:00	
10:30	
11:00	
11:30	
12:00	
12:30	
1:00	
1:30	
2:00	
2:30	
3:00	
3:30	
4:00	
4:30	
5:00	
5:30	
6:00	
6:30	
7:00	
7:30	
8:00	
8:30	
9:00	
9:30	

End of Day Reflection:

What were your wins today?

What didn't happen & why? How can you fix this moving forward?

Great work today!

Schedule your action plan for tomorrow. →

My Brilliant Ideas or Notes

DAILY ACTION PLAN

DAY 89 OF 90

Date: _____

Morning Review

In 2-days I will: _____
My #1 focus today: _____
I'm grateful for: _____

SUCCESS LIST
3 THINGS I MUST DO TODAY
Do the least desired task first!

◊ _____
◊ _____
◊ _____

◆◆◆◆◆ OTHER TO-DO'S ◆◆◆◆◆
◊ _____
◊ _____
◊ _____
◊ _____

◆◆◆◆◆ TASKS TO DELEGATE ◆◆◆◆◆
◊ _____
◊ _____
◊ _____

◆◆◆◆◆ HABITS ◆◆◆◆◆
◊ Visualized My Goal
◊ Exercised
◊ 8 Glasses of Water
♡ ♡ ♡ ♡ ♡ ♡ ♡ ♡
◊ _____
◊ _____
◊ _____

SCHEDULE

4:00
4:30
5:00
5:30
6:00
6:30
7:00
7:30
8:00
8:30
9:00
9:30
10:00
10:30
11:00
11:30
12:00
12:30
1:00
1:30
2:00
2:30
3:00
3:30
4:00
4:30
5:00
5:30
6:00
6:30
7:00
7:30
8:00
8:30
9:00
9:30

End of Day Reflection:

What were your wins today?

What didn't happen & why? How can you fix this moving forward?

Great work today!

Schedule your action plan for tomorrow. →

My Brilliant Ideas or Notes

DAILY ACTION PLAN

DAY 90 OF 90!

Date: _____

Morning Review

Today I will: _____
My #1 focus today: _____
I'm grateful for: _____

SUCCESS LIST
3 THINGS I MUST DO TODAY
Do the least desired task first!

◊ _____
◊ _____
◊ _____

✦✦✦✦ OTHER TO-DO'S ✦✦✦✦
◊ _____
◊ _____
◊ _____
◊ _____

✦✦✦✦ TASKS TO DELEGATE ✦✦✦✦
◊ _____
◊ _____
◊ _____

✦✦✦✦ HABITS ✦✦✦✦
◊ Visualized My Goal
◊ Exercised
◊ 8 Glasses of Water
♡ ♡ ♡ ♡ ♡ ♡ ♡ ♡
◊ _____
◊ _____
◊ _____

SCHEDULE

4:00
4:30
5:00
5:30
6:00
6:30
7:00
7:30
8:00
8:30
9:00
9:30
10:00
10:30
11:00
11:30
12:00
12:30
1:00
1:30
2:00
2:30
3:00
3:30
4:00
4:30
5:00
5:30
6:00
6:30
7:00
7:30
8:00
8:30
9:00
9:30

End of Day Reflection:

What were your wins today?

What didn't happen & why? How can you fix this moving forward?

Great work girl!

You completed the challenge! Let's Celebrate →

My Brilliant Ideas or Notes

SECTION 8

Celebrate You

> "One of the greatest gifts you receive when you accomplish a goal is the confirmation that you <u>can</u> achieve what you once believed was impossible."

-ROSEANNE BAKER

#GlamifyYourGoal

CELEBRATING YOUR JOURNEY

Success! You've just completed the ninety-day challenge! Bust out your sparkly party dress and toss the confetti high into the air—because this is a celebration! Please excuse all the exclamation points, but I'm *soooo* excited for you!!!! I know that you worked *extremely* hard and had to step outside your comfort zone to make things happen. How did you do, gorgeous? Whether you completed your goal 100% or not, I want you to take a bit of time to reflect and honor your achievements.

IN NINETY DAYS I...

What were your wins? List everything—things big and small.

_____
_____
_____
_____
_____
_____
_____
_____
_____
_____
_____
_____
_____
_____

THE AMAZING THING THAT I DISCOVERED ABOUT MYSELF WAS...

_____
_____
_____
_____
_____

I'M MOST PROUD OF MYSELF FOR...

_____
_____
_____
_____
_____

THE SCARIEST THING I DID WAS...

_____
_____
_____
_____
_____

THE GREATEST OBSTACLE THAT I OVERCAME WAS...

_____
_____
_____
_____
_____

I'M TRANSFORMED BY...

_____
_____
_____
_____
_____
_____
_____
_____
_____

I FEEL...

_____
_____
_____

THE NEXT GOAL I WILL ACCOMPLISH IS...

_____
_____
_____

DATE I'M GOING TO START WORKING ON THIS GOAL IS...

_____

WHAT HAPPENS NOW?

You just completed an incredible journey, but it doesn't end here. Five things you can do now are:

1. Visit http://breakthroughempire.com/glamifybonuses to share your story and get bonuses that go with this book.

2. Do you know someone who can benefit from this book? Tell them about it–you might forever change their life!

3. If you liked this book please help spread the word by posting a review on Amazon.com, or your blog, or by creating a video review on YouTube.

4. Reward yourself for a job well done—buy that handbag you've been eyeing for months, book an all-day spa treatment, or take a trip to the mountains!

5. Plan your next glamorous goal, gorgeous!

I hope this book helped you achieve your goal faster than you thought possible, that you learned a lot about yourself, and that it uplifted your life in some fashion. Always remember that your future is in your hands and you can be, do, or have anything that you want as long as you make a written plan and take action!

Live with passion, be true to you, and may all your dreams become a reality,

xx *Roseanne*

SECTION 9

Surprise! There's More

Create your own inspirational quote or write a favorite quote here!

Space for your brilliant notes, doodles, and infinite possibilities

Space for your brilliant notes, doodles, and infinite possibilities

Space for your brilliant notes, doodles, and infinite possibilities

Space for your brilliant notes, doodles, and infinite possibilities

Space for your brilliant notes, doodles, and infinite possibilities

Made in the USA
Middletown, DE
07 July 2025